T0358714

(Re)Inventing the Internet

(RE)INVENTING THE INTERNET

Critical Case Studies

Edited by

Andrew Feenberg
Simon Fraser University, Burnaby, Canada

Norm Friesen
Thompson Rivers University, Kamloops, Canada

SENSE PUBLISHERS
ROTTERDAM/BOSTON/TAIPEI

A C.I.P. record for this book is available from the Library of Congress.

ISBN: 978-94-6091-732-5 (paperback)
ISBN: 978-94-6091-733-2 (hardback)
ISBN: 978-94-6091-734-9 (e-book)

Published by: Sense Publishers,
P.O. Box 21858,
3001 AW Rotterdam,
The Netherlands
www.sensepublishers.com

Printed on acid-free paper

TABLE OF CONTENTS

PREFACE

The Internet, as Though Agency Mattered

The critique of technological determinism is something of an chapter of faith in studies of communication technologies today, thanks to two key developments dating from the early days of new media research. The first was a shift toward constructivist views of technology, borrowed from science and technology studies and cultural analyses of media in the work of Raymond Williams and others. The second was the turn toward subjectivist epistemologies and qualitative fieldwork methods that transformed communication and mass media research in the 1980s, and which encouraged a reorientation of media studies toward the "domestic" and "everyday life" contexts of media use. Since that time, media studies, cultural studies, and new media scholars have routinely disavowed the channel-centric, powerful-effects view of communication technology that pervaded so much of mass media research through the 20th century, in favour of culturally-situated, subjectively-experienced accounts of media development and use.

But if new media scholarship eschews powerful *technologies*, the field still clings to a widespread, if implicit, belief in powerful media *representations*, *content* and *institutions*. Producers and owners of media programs and systems (including new media) are assumed to wield globalized, hegemonic, and disproportionate power over consumers (even in their new guise as "users"). Although it rejects technological determinism, the field seems reluctant to part with structural/cultural determinism and the presumed "impacts" of media representations and institutions *on* individuals, society and culture. Too often, people's engagement with media is still conceptualized in terms of reception and consumption, rather than expression, organization, relations, and interaction – what elsewhere I have described as *mediation*, in both the technological sense of devices that extend our abilities to communicate, and the relational sense of negotiation and intercession (Lievrouw, 2011).

Into this arena, Andrew Feenberg and his collaborators bring a welcome, and overdue, shift of focus. Their key insight is that most media researchers, including new media scholars, have misunderstood the characteristics of networked computing and telecommunications that make "the Internet" – actually a constellation of interlinked and emergent platforms, uses, devices, affordances, and social/cultural resources and relations – a fundamentally different context and scaffolding for human communication than was ever possible via conventional mass media systems. Consequently, media researchers have tended to underestimate or even disparage the avenues and opportunities for resistance, democratic participation, and emancipatory change available via new media, and to overstate the ability of powerful institutions to block or constrain the ways that people use and reconfigure the technologies.

Certainly, new media can be used simply as pipelines for content distribution and delivery, and as with mass media distribution channels, those pipelines may be just as easy to interrupt or shut down (at least until users figure out a work-around). However, the authors in this collection argue that the real power of the Internet, as demonstrated from the earliest email programs on the ARPANET to contemporary Twitter feeds, derives from the fact that computer networking, as Feenberg puts it in his introduction, "is in fact the first successful mediation of small group activity."[1] As a communication medium, networked computing is extraordinarily well-suited to group processes and interaction, and indeed allows "local" group processes and network relations to expand to global scale. The facilitation of interpersonal and group communication, where people are *agents* and *actors* and not simply consumers of media products, is the source of the persistent appeal and power of new media.

Moreover, the material infrastructure of the Internet and related technologies is, as Feenberg says, "radically incomplete," not yet approaching the kind of closure and stabilization that have marked communication technologies in the past. (Indeed, I would go further and argue that Internet design and architecture, predicated on "survivability," redundancy, and openness to diverse devices and applications, actually *resist* this type of closure. The "recombinant" quality of Internet infrastructure is what allows us to keep calling new media "new" [Lievrouw & Livingstone, 2006]). This persistent lack of closure, and the incompleteness, emergence, or recombinant dynamics of new media technologies, in some sense invite people to tinker with existing features and platforms, and use them to devise new or non-obvious affordances and uses according to their own purposes and interests. Feenberg, of course, has usefully theorized this process, within his broader critical theory of technology, as *instrumentalization*: people seeking solutions to problems recognize potentially useful objects and affordances in the world, remove them from their original settings and purposes to highlight their new uses, and then reconfigure and fit them back into existing systems, standards, and repertoires of practice in new ways (Feenberg, 2005).

Together, the ability of Internet infrastructure to support and extend group interaction, and its "radical incompleteness," have fostered a diversified, idiosyncratic, opportunistic and serendipitous arena for building relationships, interaction and what Feenberg calls "new forms of agency." Actors can use technology to challenge established institutional power and prerogatives, and in the process reconfigure not only the prevailing social order, but the technical infrastructure that supports and subtends it. New forms of agency have opened the way for the new, mediated modes of sociality, reciprocity, participation, mobilization, and resistance that are highlighted in this book.

The chapters and cases collected here provide rich evidence that agency and action are key to understanding people's engagement with new media. To mention just a few examples: Bakardjieva documents the "subactivism" of people with little time for institutional politics, but who nonetheless identify with one another and cultivate their "small world" interests and concerns interpersonally, online. Subactivism thus echoes the "unconventional action repertoires" and "prefigurative" forms of political action described by theorists of new social movements (i.e., movement members "live" their politics through their lifestyles, identities, creative works, and relationships, rather than joining formal political organizations and campaigns). But Bakardjieva's findings demonstrate the inseparability of such activities in online and offline modes of everyday life.

Hamilton and Feenberg make the case that effective online teaching, like effective face-to-face instruction, is fundamentally relational and not merely a matter of information delivery. Understood this way, online pedagogy has the potential to enrich and extend the traditional values of scholarship and teaching, and to resist the deskilling and reduction of higher education to David Noble's feared "digital diploma mills." Friesen, Feenberg and Smith call for a move away from framing surveillance in Foucauldian, "panoptic" terms that emphasize the unseen power embodied in remote databases, and toward a framework that recognizes people's own power to understand, act on, and undermine the interests of surveilling interests and advance their own. This notion of surveilled persons as subjective, and active, agents and actors, rather than acted-upon "representations," is broadly congruent with much recent work in surveillance studies that emphasizes "ethical surveillance" and people's capabilities to recognize, resist, and even play with the information that they reveal about themselves and thus subvert institutional aims and power (Monahan, Murikami-Woods & Phillips, 2010; boyd, 2011).

This collection, then, is not just a set of empirical "tests" of the critical theory of technology. More importantly, it is another step in the movement in new media scholarship toward an understanding of communication technologies as inextricably entwined in everyday experience, and of mediated communication as a complex, contingent and continuous process that articulates the symbolic and the material, technology and experience, structure and action, constraint and agency.

NOTES

[1] The extensive literature on computer mediated communication [CMC], grounded in theories of interpersonal, small group, and organizational communication rather than mass communication research, richly demonstrates the power of this insight. (See, e.g., Thurlow, Lengel & Tomic, 2004.)

REFERENCES

Boyd, B. (2011). Dear voyeur, meet flâneur…sincerely, social media. *Surveillance & Society, 8*(4), 505–507.

Feenberg, A. (2005). Critical theory of technology: An overview. *Tailoring Biotechnologies, 1*(1), 47–64.

Lievrouw, L. A. (2011). *Alternative and activist new media.* Cambridge: Polity.

Lievrouw, L. A. & Livingstone, S. (2006). Introduction to the updated student edition. In L. A. Lievrouw & S. Livingstone (Eds.) *The handbook of new media* (updated student edition). London: Sage.

PREFACE

Monahan, T., Murikami-Wood, D. & Phillips, D. J. (Eds.) (2010). Special issue on surveillance and empowerment. *Surveillance & Society, 8*(2).

Thurlow, C., Lengel, L. & Tomic, A. (2004). *Computer-mediated communication: Social interaction and the Internet.* Thousand Oaks, CA: Sage.

Leah A. Lievrouw
Los Angeles, 2011

I. CODE AND COMMUNICATION

ANDREW FEENBERG

INTRODUCTION

Toward a Critical Theory of the Internet

Technologies normally stabilize after an initial period during which many differing configurations compete. Once stabilized, their social and political implications finally become clear. But despite decades of development, the Internet remains in flux as innovative usages continue to appear. The nature of the network is still in question. It is not a fully developed technology like the refrigerator or the ball point pen. Yet this has not prevented a huge outpouring of literature hyping the Internet or criticizing its impact. Some point to the empowering effects of online activity on recent electoral campaigns in the US and revolts in the Arab world to argue that the Internet is a democratizing force. Others claim that the Internet is just a virtual mall, a final extension of capitalist rationalization into every corner of our lives, a trend supported by an ever denser web of surveillance technologies threatening individual autonomy and democratic discourse. In fact this controversy is the best evidence that the Internet is not a finished work. The case cannot be closed while the debate continues with such fierce intensity.

This book offers an original approach to the controversy. Each of the five chapters acknowledge the intensified rationalization brought about by the Internet while also highlighting the innovative forms of community that emerge among the publics these technologies assemble.

Communities of medical patients, video game players, musicians and their audiences, and many other groups have emerged on the Internet with surprising consequences. This introduction will focus on the significance of such communities as sites of resistance. Although they appear marginal to politics in the usual sense, they are redefining the political in response to the omnipresence of technology. The correlation of technological rationalization and democratic social initiative provides a more complete picture of the Internet than either aspect taken by itself.

The critical theory of technology, applied in some measure in each of the chapters, emphasizes the political structuring of the world emerging under the impact of the Internet. Technology is neither a realm of rational consensus nor is it a mere tool of its owners and managers. We have learned from social studies of science and technology (STS) that technology assembles workers, users, even victims, who share in common a world it creates. Their participation in these technological worlds shapes their conception of their concerns and channels their activities. Yet this is not a deterministic thesis. Technology is not an independent variable but is "co-constructed" by the social forces it organizes and unleashes.

Critical theory of technology departs from mainstream STS in treating such technological worlds as terrains of struggle on which hegemonic forces express

A. Feenberg and N. Friesen (eds.), (Re)Inventing the Internet: Critical Case Studies, 3–17.
© *2012 Sense Publishers. All rights reserved.*

themselves through specific design strategies in opposition to subordinate groups that are more or less successful in influencing the future form of the artifacts with which they are engaged. The Internet enables communication among these subordinate groups with significant effects. In the chapters that follow, these abstract methodological principles are applied to concrete cases involving surveillance, online education, video games, Internet activism, and citizenship.[1]

HISTORICAL BACKGROUND

The earliest version of what has become the Internet went online in 1969. This system was called the ARPANET, after the Advanced Research Projects Agency of the defense department that specialized in "blue sky" projects, projects so wild and speculative no normal government agency would dare fund them. It is interesting to note that even at this early stage some of the engineers involved believed their work would have enormous beneficial impacts. They prophesied a global community organized by computer networks. One of these early enthusiasts, Vinton Cerf, waxed poetic in his "Requiem for the APRANET." He wrote:

Like distant islands sundered by the sea,
we had no sense of one community.
We lived and worked apart and rarely knew
that others searched with us for knowledge, too...

But, could these new resources not be shared?
Let links be built; machines and men be paired!
Let distance be no barrier! They set
that goal: design and build the ARPANET!
(quoted in Abbate, 1994.)[2]

The Internet gradually went public in the 1980s and '90s, but even earlier social commentators were prophesying great things from computer mediated communication. In 1978 Murray Turoff and Roxanne Hiltz published a work of analysis and prediction entitled *The Network Nation* (1993). They foresaw widespread adoption of computer networking for telework and education. They believed networking would promote gender equality and speculated that electronic discussion and voting would revivify the public sphere in democratic societies.

They may have over-estimated the transformative power of their favorite technology, but their projections were modest compared to many that came afterwards. According to a whole new genre of Internet hype, networking was a change comparable in significance to the Industrial Revolution and would soon transform every aspect of our lives. Cities would be depopulated as people retreated to electronic cottages in the woods. Government as we know it would be replaced by continuous electronic plebiscites. Intelligent "agents" would learn our preferences and control the mechanical world around us without our having to lift a finger. Even sex would be transformed through remote access to virtual partners.

Naturally, the hype called forth its demystification. The historian of technology David Noble warned ominously that "visions of democratization and popular empowerment via the net are dangerous delusions; whatever the gains, they are overwhelmingly overshadowed and more than nullified by the losses. As the computer screens brighten with promise for the few, the light at the end of the tunnel grows dimmer for the many" (Noble, consulted Nov. 11, 2006: 12).

Noble expressed the widespread skepticism about the Internet that appeared in the 1990s as it became a theme of popular discussion. Social critics point to a number of phenomena inimical to democracy. Some argue that the digital divide excludes the poor while enhancing the powers of the well-to-do. Others complain that online discussion merely reinforces preexisting prejudices because people segregate themselves on the Internet from those with whom they disagree. Still others argue that the Internet is so thoroughly colonized by business that it is little more than a vehicle for advertising. Democracy is threatened by new technologies of surveillance that employ the network to concentrate information from many sources, exposing deviations from the norm through tracking and data mining.

This threat is the subject of the chapter by Norm Friesen, Andrew Feenberg, Grace Chung and Shannon Lowe. The chapter explores the consequences of surveillance for personal identity and the resistance it evokes. The chapter notes that surveillance technology gives rise to temporary communities of the surveilled, who enact their unruly dissent before the camera. And as Wikileaks has shown, surveillance is a two way street and can occasionally be turned against the surveillers.

The most trenchant critiques of the Internet challenge its capacity to support human community. Without face-to-face contact, it is said, people cannot take each other seriously enough to form a community. How can moral roles bind us and real consequences flow from interactions that are no more durable than a flicker on the screen? As Albert Borgmann wrote, "plugged into the network of communications and computers, people seem to enjoy omniscience and omnipotence; severed from their network, they turn out to be insubstantial and disoriented. They no longer command their world as persons in their own right. Their conversation is without depth and wit; their attention is roving and vacuous; their sense of place is uncertain and fickle" (Borgmann, 1992: 108).[3]

In this Introduction I respond to such criticisms and argue that the Internet does have democratic implications. I do not exaggerate the significance of the Internet. It will not replace Congress with a universal electronic town hall nor will it overthrow dictatorships around the world. On the other hand, the contrary exaggeration seems to me to reflect a lack of perspective. It threatens to blind us to real possibilities that should be seized rather than dismissed. These possibilities have to do with online community, supported by the Internet, and given over, as the critics note, to endless talk. But discussion lies at the heart of a democratic polity. Any new scene on which it unfolds enhances the public sphere. In an increasingly rationalized society, where individuals' activities are more and more strictly structured by business and government, the existence of this new form of community is particularly significant (Neyland and Woolgar, 2006).

Complaints about the Internet are similar to complaints about television broadcasting and in fact it seems that bad experience with the latter has shaped negative expectations about the former. Recall that television promised a "global village" (McLuhan) in which new solidarities would arise from easy access to information about other peoples and their problems. It is true that useful information circulates on the evening news but arguably propaganda and advertising have far more influence.

Aldous Huxley published *Brave New World* in the early 1930s, only a few years after the first commercial radio broadcasts, but already his dystopian vision of a totally manipulated public captured this very real threat. Many social critics seem to have concluded that technical mediation as such leads to mass alienation. Can the Internet be squeezed into this same pattern? I do not believe so.

The difference between television and the Internet is a consequence of their different technical structures. In broadcasting a single source sends out messages to a silent mass audience. Computer networking restores the normal pattern of human communication in which listening and speaking roles alternate rather than being distributed exclusively to one or another interlocutor. Furthermore, networking is the first successful technical mediation of small group activity. The telephone brought together pairs of interlocutors and broadcasting addressed mass audiences. But until recently the huge range of human activities that go on in small groups was not technically mediated and therefore could only be carried out in face-to-face settings. The Internet enables reciprocal communication among small groups. The members of these groups both receive and emit information. This is an important advance that we tend to take for granted since it seems so obvious after 30 years of widespread online communication.

The critics underestimate this phenomenon and respond more to the exaggerated claims of Internet hype than to the reality of online experience, including even their own. For example, in a recent chapter in *The New Yorker,* Malcolm Gladwell compares the Internet unfavorably with sit ins in the civil rights movement (Gladwell, 2010). How much courage does it take, he asks, to sign an Internet petition? This is silly. It would make more sense to compare the Internet with the telephone trees and mimeograph machines we used to notify activists and print up leaflets back in the days of the sit ins rather than the political acts those means of communication were intended to serve.

Here is another case in point. Hubert Dreyfus focuses his critique of the Internet on a group called the Extropians who look forward to the day their brains can be downloaded into computers (Dreyfus, 2001). There would be no point in attacking this group if it were not significant, but I do not see what it can signify to those of us who use the Internet daily while remaining firmly committed to embodied existence. To confuse matters further, Dreyfus dodges the charge of Luddism at the end of his book by explaining his use of the Internet in his classes at Berkeley. Nowhere does he reflect on the social and political significance of online community. Instead, he actually dismisses online discussion as trivial because it is not carried on with sufficient expertise or commitment. But that is not so much a critique of the Internet as of democracy itself.

Missing in the critics' account is any sense of the great victory represented by the conquest of this new territory for ordinary human communication. There is a long history of communication technologies introduced for broadcasting or official usages that ended up as instruments of informal human interaction. The telephone, for example, was originally intended for government business. When women appropriated it to organize the social life of their families, engineers complained bitterly about the waste of their beautiful instrument (Fischer, 1988). Even more surprising, the telephone was at first imagined as a broadcasting technology. In the early days, several companies distributed live musical performances to subscribers. In France the Théâtrophone company thrived until 1920 broadcasting operas (Bertho, 1984: 80–81).

This pattern is repeated in the case of computer networking. The first successful domestic network was not the Internet but the French Minitel system. Concerned about the slowness of computerization in France, the government established a network based on technology similar to that of the Internet. Six million free Minitel terminals were distributed to telephone subscribers in the early 1980s. These terminals were designed to consult a national electronic phone directory, to display news and classified ads, to consult train schedules, examination results, and other official documents. But soon after the system was deployed hackers introduced instant messaging. It did not take long for this unexpected application to become the Minitel's single most important usage. Ironically most of the messaging was dedicated to the search for dates and sex. The cool new information medium was transformed into a hot electronic singles bar (Feenberg, 2010: chap. 5).

Like the Minitel network, the Internet was not originally designed to support human communication and it could have excluded the public entirely. Given its military origins, this might well have been the outcome. But the technology underlying the Internet is so powerful it could hardly be contained. This technology, called packet switching, is useful among other things for building a secure communication system. This is what originally interested the military. The telephone network is vulnerable because it depends on a central computer to connect up correspondents. A single bomb could take out the whole system by hitting this center, but packet switching makes it possible to route messages through many different computers and so the system does not depend on the survival of any one of its nodes. Strange as it seems today, radio communication among tank commanders was suggested as an early application of packet switching.

Military planners were more interested in survivability than control. For this reason their design was non-hierarchical and redundant, qualities that later turned out to privilege the free flow of information and innovation. Features of the original design persist and pose significant problems for business and repressive governments while also enabling both public spirited and socially stigmatized activities to go on unhindered. The military design of the Internet thus comes to the aid of ordinary users (Abbate, 1999).

The early ARPANET was intended to test the new technology with university based military researchers. After World War II, military planners were convinced that American power depended on scientific research, and they believed the scientists who told them that research depended on communication and collaboration. The

Pentagon hoped that university scientists would share computing resources and data over the Internet.

Soon after the ARPANET went online, at a time when it connected only a few universities, an engineer introduced an e-mail program. Like the early telephone company engineers, those responsible for the ARPANET project were at first leery of wasteful socializing but they soon came to appreciate its potential for building community and so they allowed the experiment in e-mail to continue. We have inherited the consequence of that decision.

To get an idea of its significance imagine how we would feel if institutions such as universities, government agencies, and corporations allowed only official communication on their property: no jokes, no personal remarks, no criticism. We would surely find such severe censorship totalitarian. The Internet could have been configured technically in just this way. The result would have been the enhancement of official communication in business and government with no corresponding enhancement of the informal communication in which daily life goes on, including the conversations of political significance that form the basis of the democratic public sphere.

This hypothetical example indicates the need for a different approach to understanding the Internet from that taken by its severest critics. They focus on the triviality of most of the communications but they fail to realize that without opening a channel for trivial speech, there can be no serious speech. We have no record of the conversations in those 18th and 19th century pubs and coffee houses idealized (perhaps rightly) as the birthplaces of the public sphere, but no doubt in their precincts much time was wasted. Rather than comparing the Internet unfavorably with edited cultural products like newspapers, it would make more sense to compare it with the social interactions that take place on the street. There the coexistence of the good, the bad and the trivial is normal, not an offense to taste or intellectual standards because we have no expectation of uniform quality. In what follows I will outline an approach that allows for the dross and also the gold in the flood of words on the Internet.

I intend to do this through a brief account of the public role of online community on the Internet. I will not discuss the myriad examples of democratic politics in the usual sense of the term. The list of activities in which the Internet plays a role gets longer every year, starting with the Zapatista movement in Mexico and continuing with the protests against the WTO and the IMF, and the world wide demonstrations against the War in Iraq. The Internet also plays an important role in electoral politics, first coming to attention with Howard Dean's campaign and finally paying off in the election of Barack Obama. The recent Arab revolts should be proof enough of the political potential of the Internet. In all these cases the Internet has broken the near monopoly of the business and government dominated official press and television networks by enabling activists to organize and to speak directly to millions of Internet users (Mccaughey and Ayers, 2003).

These examples seem to me to provide strong evidence for my position, but they are not enough for Darin Barney, who argues that "these alternative and resistant practices still represent a tear in a salty sea of hegemonic encounters with the broad scope of digital technology and its culture. To take the measure of the present conjuncture we need careful work that documents and even promotes tactical political uses of these technologies, but we also need to place these uses in the broader context of what remains a very powerful set of technologies configured to advance and secure what Jacques Rancière has described as the 'unlimited power of wealth'" (Barney, 2011).

To answer objections such as this, a theoretical framework must give the political Internet substance. After all, as Barney suggests, political usages might be exceptional and the Internet defined by narcissistic self-advertisement and business. My main concern in what follows is to develop a coherent alternative to such critical assessments. To anticipate my conclusion, I argue that politics on the Internet is the tip of the iceberg, arising in the midst of a broader revival of agency in many different types of online communities, and that it deserves our full attention and, indeed, our support.

TECHNOLOGY IN FLUX

I want to begin by introducing some essential methodological considerations. As I noted at the beginning of this Introduction, it is a commonplace error to consider the Internet finished and complete before it has actually achieved its final shape. Critics repeatedly generalize from rapidly changing characteristics to timeless conclusions soon outdated by further changes. But how can we evaluate a technology that is still in process, that is radically incomplete? This problem has been addressed by constructivist approaches in technology studies (Pinch and Bijker, 1987).

The chief idea shared by these approaches is negative: the success of a technology is not fully explained by its technical achievements. There are always alternative paths of development and social forces determine which are pursued and which fall by the wayside. Behind each of the technical devices that surround us there lies a ghostly halo of alternatives that were eliminated at some stage and which we have forgotten or notice only in quaint illustrations of old books. What is called the principle of "underdetermination" teaches that technical considerations alone cannot explain why we are living with this particular survivor of the process of elimination rather than that one. Historical events, not technical superiority in some absolute sense, explains why, for example, we use electric rather than gas powered refrigerators, and why our cars run on gasoline rather than kilowatts.

To make matters still more complicated, the struggle between alternatives is not a straightforward competition to achieve the same goal. Approximately the same technology, with a slightly different design, can serve the interests and needs of very different social groups. Consider, for example, the significant social difference made by such a trivial technical change as the introduction of sidewalk ramps. The rights of the disabled are embodied in those ramps. Here is another example. The early bicycle came in two main varieties, a speedy type with a large front wheel and a slower, more stable version with wheels the same size. Neither was "better" than the other. The contest between them was decided by which value, speed or stability, was to be supreme in the world of bicycles. We know which won out.

Thereafter all later evolution of the bicycle benefited the successful line of development. The defeated alternative was left frozen in time like a dinosaur fossil and so appears obviously inferior today in a typical illusion of progress.

The ambiguity of the early bicycle is typical. It illustrates what constructivists call the "interpretive flexibility" of technologies. Until it is clear what a technology is for, its design cannot be standardized. Technologies are most ambiguous at the beginning of their development when several designs compete. Eventually one among these designs wins out and a standard emerges. The standard usually prevails for a long time, but it can be unseated and interpretive flexibility return if the conditions that favored it change. We are surrounded by such stabilized technologies, but the Internet is not yet among them. It is still in the full flush of its early development and so is radically indeterminate.

This constructivist approach represents technologies not as things but as processes in more or less rapid movement. The process pulls at first in several different directions but is finally stabilized in a single more or less durable form. Because our lives move quickly with respect to these stabilized forms, it appears that technical artifacts are finished and fixed rather than relatively temporary arrangements that may enter into flux again at a future date. We assume the functions they serve are the obvious ones similar technologies ought to serve rather than noticing the contingency of their functions on particular configurations of social forces that interpreted the problems in a certain way at the outset. Constructivism aims to overcome this illusion in order to restore a more accurate picture of the process of development.

To apply the constructivist approach to the Internet, we need to identify the various versions of it that currently coexist and from among which a selection will finally be made. Note that the closure of the Internet around one of these possible configurations does not preclude the survival of the others in subordinate roles. At its inception radio broadcasting was dominated by education and public programming and television was originally conceived for surveillance and education. Both technologies quickly fell under the control of business and are defined today as entertainment media. Other usages were not excluded although the technical and legal dimensions of these alternatives are largely determined by the requirements of entertainment (McChesney, 1999).

Critics of the Internet believe something similar has already happened, but they exaggerate the extent of business control so far achieved. A truly business oriented network like the Minitel offers possibilities unthinkable on the Internet. For example, the French system was designed to track the time individual users spent on services so as to charge them by the minute through their telephone bill. The network protocol employed by the French Telecom made this possible while also complicating the internationalization of the system. The Internet protocol is not able reliably to charge users for services, hence the importance of advertising, but it has other features which have enabled it to spread over the entire globe. Business is a latecomer to this global system and it is still struggling to impose its hegemony.

THREE MODELS

I have argued that the Internet is still in flux, wavering between alternative paths of development. I identify three possible paths for the Internet which I call "models" since they aspire to define the dominant features of the technology. Each of these models represents a possible configuration that may prevail in the future. They are: the *information* model, the *consumption* model, and the *community* model. As we will see only the community model bears the democratic potential of the Internet.

The Information Model

This model presided over the origins of the Internet and similar systems such as the Minitel network in France. It aims at improving the distribution of information, a function that the Internet fulfills and will undoubtedly continue to fulfill so long as it exists. As a social project computer networking was intended to realize sociological theories of the information age according to which knowledge has replaced industry as the most important source of wealth and power. The information model realizes this vision by offering wide access to information. This is what inspired attempts to spread the information model from professional into domestic settings in the 1980s in France and a decade later on the Internet. In fact it quickly became apparent that personal communication was far more attractive to users of these systems than any economically significant exchange of information. Thus the information model has little chance to prevail as an overall interpretation of the meaning of the Internet.

The consumption model

It is a curious and little known fact that the early Internet was virulently hostile to business. Attempts to sell goods and services on the system were severely repressed. An individual who scandalized the community by engaging in commercial activity would be attacked by hundreds, even thousands, of hostile emails. But once the decision was made in the early 1990s to allow commercial activity on the Internet, a tidal wave of corporate initiatives swept over the rather sedate virtual space occupied up to then by individual hobbyists and university faculty. The Internet was the technology behind the famous dotcom boom and even the later bust did not diminish the pace of business activity in cyberspace for long. Today, Internet-based markets are a factor in the prosperity of nations.

This new type of market inexpensively links up people and goods over a global territory. The most profitable Internet businesses resemble eBay in stocking little or no inventory, but in delivering a smooth connection between supply and demand. Although email remains the most used function of the Internet, e-business does not lag far behind.

The consumption model has enormous potential for growth because film and television have not yet been fully adapted for delivery over the Internet. We can expect a huge boost in consumption usages when every sort of recorded entertainment is readily available. Already this prospect is pressing on the legislative agenda of the United States government. Entertainment companies and Internet service providers are anxious to obtain the legal right to convert the Internet into an enhanced version of television by privileging high speed delivery of entertainment over other functions served by the system.

This means the end of "network neutrality," the current rule under which all types of communication are treated equally. If the companies prevail, the Internet may soon see far less communicative and public usages as bandwidth is monopolized by profit making enterprise. While so far this is primarily an American debate, its effects would be felt worldwide, as was the case with the Digital Millennium Copyright Act. Further development of the technology would undoubtedly follow along lines determined in the US for years to come. The triumph of the consumption model would transform both the dominant interpretation of the system and its technology.

The community model

The Internet as we know it today is dominated not by business but by users whose free communication prevails in cyberspace. The two main types of personal communication are individual email and various forms of group communication such as listservs, computer conferences and web forums. Initially, these were separate from homepages, which contained personal information. This has changed as communication and personal content are combined on social sites such as Myspace, Facebook, and Blogs, often referred to collectively as Web 2.0.[4] Communities form around these spaces of virtual social interaction.

Community is the primary scene of human communication and personal development. It is in this context that people judge the world around them and discuss their judgments with others. Any technology that offers new possibilities for the formation of community is thus democratically significant.

But are online communities real communities, engaging their members seriously? The testimony of participants as well as extensive research confirms that the Internet is the scene of new forms of sociability that strongly resemble face-to-face community. For example, surveys conducted in several countries by Japanese researchers reveal that the ethical assumptions guiding Internet users resemble their everyday ethical behaviors (Nara and Iseda, 2004). Not technology but character determines behavior online. And character is precisely what community requires, i.e. the ability to commit to a group of fellow human beings. The behaviors and symbols that sustain and support the imagined unity of community are routinely reproduced on the Internet. I cannot pursue this argument further here but there is much more to say in defense of the idea of online community (Feenberg and Bakardjieva, 2004).

The essence of the community model is reciprocity. Each participant is both reader or viewer and publisher. To maintain this structure, the community model requires the continued neutrality of the network so that non-professional, unprofitable and politically controversial communication will not be marginalized. It must be possible to introduce innovative designs for new forms of association without passing through bureaucratic or commercial gatekeepers. The involvement of open source developers and other unpaid volunteers is essential and cannot be expected to survive a commercial take-over of cyberspace. Embedding a strict regime of intellectual property in the technology of the system would surely be incompatible with free communicative interaction.

The conditions of community are both social and technical. Should the community model prevail, commercial, entertainment and informational applications would certainly find their place, but they could not dominate the evolution of the system with their special technical requirements. Indeed, so far business seems to be adapting to the requirements of community: the commercial takeover of certain community sites turns them into platforms for advertising without necessarily disturbing their communicative content.

The relations between these three models are complex, characterized by elements of conflict as well as innovative combinations of features drawn from each. Two chapters of this book, on online education and video games, illustrate the complexity that results from their interaction.

The chapter by Hamilton and Feenberg describes the development of online education since its invention in the early 1980s. Only online discussion was possible then and so a pedagogy developed based on dialogue and collaboration. Later, university administrations were attracted by the still unfulfilled promise of automated learning on the Internet. The collapse of that project has left a confusing situation in which online education means very different things to different people. Millions of students use online sites and forums today. Many of them are adult learners who would not be able to study in a traditional university setting. The communicative potential of online education represents a great improvement over the one way model of traditional distance learning. For on-campus students, online education offers opportunities for discussion as a supplement to lectures held in a conventional classroom setting. This too seems an improvement over the traditional lecture course. Nevertheless, there is a risk that because it is a new and poorly understood technology, online education will provide a cover for the reduction of education to the mechanical delivery of materials. The struggle over the future of the Internet is paralleled by this controversy over how best to employ it in education, either to constitute educational communities or to distribute information or, most likely, some combination of the two models.

The video game industry offers another example of the complex interactions that characterize the Internet today. The industry is now larger than Hollywood and engages millions of subscribers in online multiplayer games. The players' gaming activities are structured by the game code, but online communities organize them in informal relationships that the industry does not control. The "ludification theory" presented in the chapter by Grimes and Feenberg explains how these communities form within and in reaction to the rationalized structures of game technology. Once activated, the community struggles to reconfigure aspects of the game, mobilizing code and items from the game in new ways and contexts. Markets appear in goods won during play as players auction them off for money. Games are modified by players skilled at hacking. Companies may protest these unauthorized activities but in the end they usually give in and attempt to co-opt what they cannot control. Interaction between game designers and players and among the players themselves creates an environment unlike the mass audiences created by television broadcasting.

THE POLITICAL INTERNET

Commentators noted early that online communities form around a shared interest or concern. In this they differ from geographically based communities in which a far more mixed population is related by place. Is this good or bad? Disadvantaged publics can pool their forces online and have a greater impact. This has made it possible for ordinary Americans to raise huge sums of money for political candidates who might have been swamped at the polls by adversaries with the support of a few wealthy contributors or party organizations. On the other hand, public debate involves disagreement and it is said that debate is sidetracked by the homogeneity of Internet groups. Yet it is by no means certain that people engage in livelier exchanges off-line. In any case, those interested in politics rarely confine all their political conversation to the Internet. Everyone has many face-to-face contacts in which the opportunity for disagreement arises. This is not a persuasive reason to condemn the Internet and all its works.

These familiar debates overlook a more important issue. The most innovative democratic implications of the Internet are only beginning to emerge, and they have less to do with traditional politics than with new forms of agency that will redefine and enlarge the sphere of politics. What we commonly identify as politics on the Internet is merely an instance of this broader phenomenon. To understand this new politics we will need to reconsider how we think about technology once more.

Until recently, the main emphasis in discussions of technology has been on efficiency, but American philosophers of technology argue that this is insufficient. Langdon Winner was among the first to argue that "artifacts have politics" and to suggest that technology imposes a quasi-constitutional regime in laying out the conditions of everyday life (Winner, 1986: 47ff). Lawrence Lessig similarly proposes that "code is law" (Lessig, 2011). But while technology has such legislative power, it also shares the defect of much legislation in favoring some interests at the expense of others. This is why it would be desirable to establish a more democratic technological regime, enabling the representation of a broad array of interests.

But politics differs from technology in many ways. Political representation in democratic republics has always been organized primarily around geographical units. The common interests of those who live together provide a basis for shared decisions and the choice of representatives. Where disagreements arise, they can be overcome through discussion and voting in a community forum or election of some sort.

Representation is the principal means of community self-assertion in modern democracies. It is through their representatives that groups pursue their interests in the political sphere. We call this exercise of power "agency," meaning the capacity to act. Representatives in traditional politics exert agency on behalf of a community, acting more or less under its control.

But advanced technological societies assemble collectives of geographically scattered individuals around technical mediations of one sort or another. Educational activities, work, entertainment, even illness create a shared world in which the individuals circulate just as much as they do in their local community. New networks emerge that are mediated by shared relations to technology and these networks overlay the geographical communities and compete with them in significance in the lives of citizens. To belong to such a network is to have specific interests that flow from participation in the opportunities it opens up and the problems it causes. I call these "participant interests." They may be represented better or worse depending on the design and organization of the network, the possibilities it offers for its members to recognize their shared belonging, and the body of knowledge that presides over it (Feenberg, 1999: chap. 6).

The Internet has the power to put those involved in these technically mediated networks in contact with each other. What is most innovative and politically significant about the Internet is its capacity to support collective reflection on participant interests. This is the central theme of Bakardjieva's contribution to this book. She explains the emergence of new forms of community among Internet users in response to a wide array of civic problems and frustrations. Bakardjieva calls this "subactivism," a kind of pre-politics that opens spaces for agency in relation to institutions such as the medical system, government agencies, and schools. The boundaries between the personal and the political, the "small world" of everyday life and the larger society are shifting.

The representation of technically mediated communities is complicated by the role of experts in the creation and operation of technical networks (Feenberg, 1995: chap. 5). Experts represent the community constituted by a technical network in the sense that they implement some of the participant interests of its members. But expertise is based on technical knowledge which, unlike the wisdom sought in political representatives, is cumulative and must be acquired through extensive training. Like technologies, technical disciplines are underdetermined and realize specific social interests in technically rational forms. These bodies of technical knowledge transmitted to successive generations of experts contain the outcome of past struggles over design. Current designs are responsive to this technical inheritance and to the agency of current participants bringing pressure to bear on those in control of technology.

Where technology is involved the enormous cost and the long time delays in generating a cadre of experts forbid abrupt and drastic changes. As new groups emerge, they must impress their concerns on a body of experts, convince them to modify existing designs, and eventually install their concerns in the training of the next generation of experts. The participant interests of members of technically mediated communities are thus represented differently from political interests of geographically based communities.

In her chapter, Milberry discusses this problem as it has been addressed by the new "tech activism." The emergence of a cohort of self-taught radical experts on the technology of the Internet opens up new possibilities. Milberry examines how and why these tech activists appropriated wiki technology, using it as a space and tool for democratic communication in cyberspace. In turn, this has enabled the realization of new communicative practices offline, establishing a dialectical relation between technological experts and the social world they serve. Democratic practice online prefigures a more just society in which democratic interventions into the development and use of technology are consciously organized.

The chapters of this book show how online communities have begun to use the Internet to coordinate their demands for a fuller representation of participant interests. Despite discouraging developments in other domains, agency in the technical sphere is on the rise. New forms of online politics cannot replace traditional geographically based representation, but their existence does mean that activity in the public sphere can now extend to embrace technical issues formerly considered neutral and given over to experts to decide without consultation. This creates a social and technical environment in which agency in the traditional domains of politics has also begun to recover from the passivity induced by a steady diet of broadcasting.

The research challenges presented by this new situation are daunting. Politics is no longer the exclusive affair of traditionally constituted political groups debating the traditional issues. The range of issues and groups is constantly widening in the most unpredictable ways. New groups emerge through struggles to constitute an identity as they simultaneously work to redescribe and reinvent the "world" in which they live (Callon, et al., 2009). Internet researchers must be alert to similar phenomena in the technically mediated environment they study.

The examples described in the chapters of this book suggest a significant change in our world. The return of agency may appear non-political but what is democracy if not the activity of individuals in determining their own collective life? And to the extent that so much of life is now mediated by technology, more and more of it becomes available for these new forms of community control. That is, if the community model is able to sustain itself. This is the ultimate challenge for online community: to preserve the conditions of community on the Internet. A democratic Internet? That depends on the capacity of ordinary users to defend its democratic potential in the coming years.

NOTES

[1] For a review of the relation between media theory and STS, see Boczkowski and Lievrouw (2008).
[2] Fortunately, Cerf is a better engineer than poet!
[3] But for his later view, see Borgmann, (2004).
[4] It is worth noting that Web 2.0, insofar as there really is such a thing, did not introduce community to the Internet. It consists of the concretization and combination of communicative resources already present in separate programs in the online environment.

REFERENCES

Abbate, J. (1994). From Arpanet to Internet: A History of ARPA-sponsored Computer Networks, 1966–1988, unpublished Ph.D. dissertation. University of Pennsylvania.

Abbate, J. (1999). *Inventing the Internet*. Cambridge, Massachusetts: MIT Press.

Barney, D. http://figureground.ca/interviews/darin-barney/ (consulted April 14, 2011).

Bertho, C. (1984). *Histoire des telecommunications en France*. Toulouse: Editions Erès.

Boczkowski, P., Lievrouw, L. (2008). Bridging STS and communication studies: Scholarship on media and information technologies. In E. Hackett, O. Amsterdamska, M. Lynch, and J. Wajcman (Eds.), *Handbook of science and technology studies*, pp. 949–977. Cambridge, MA: MIT Press.

Borgmann, A. (1992). *Crossing the postmodern divide*. Chicago: University of Chicago Press.

Borgmann, A. (2004). Is the Internet the solution to the problem of community. In A. Feenberg & D. Barney, *Community in the digital age*. Lanham: Rowman and Littlefield.

Callon, M., Lascoumbes, P., Barthe, Y. (2009). *Acting in an uncertain world: An essay on technical democracy*. Cambridge, Mass.: MIT Press.

Dreyfus, H. (2001). *On the Internet*. London: Routledge.

Feenberg, A. (1999). *Questioning technology*. New York: Routledge.

Feenberg, A. (2010). *Between reason and experience*. Cambridge, Mass.: MIT Press.

Feenberg, A., Bakardjieva, M. (2004). Consumers or Citizens? The Online Community Debate. In A. Feenberg & D. Barney, *Community in the digital age*. Lanham: Rowman and Littlefield.

Fischer, C. (1988). "Touch Someone:" The telephone industry discovers sociability. Technology and Culture 29.

Gladwell, M. (2010). "Why the revolution will not be tweeted." *The New Yorker*, October 4.

Hiltz, S. R., Turoff, M. (1993). *The network nation*. Cambridge: MIT Press.

Lessig, L. (2006). *Code: and other laws of Cyberspace Version 2.0*. New York: Basic Books.

McCaughey, M., Ayers, M. (2003). *Cyberactivism: Online activism in theory and practice*. New York: Routledge.

McChesney, R. (1999). *Rich media, poor democracy: Communication politics in dubious times*. Urbana and Chicago: University of Illinois Press.

Milberry, K. (2007). The wiki way: Prefiguring change, practicing democracy. *Tailoring Biotechnologies*, (3)1.

Neyland, D., Woolgar, S. (2006). "Governance and Accountability Relations in Mundane Techno-Scientific Solutions to Public Problems," http://www.sci-soc.net/NR/rdonlyres/D6219271-2604-4B20-820D-4C88F8B76AC2/811/Governanceandaccountability.pdf (consulted Dec. 2, 2008).

Noble, D. The Truth about the Information Highway.

http://www/arise.org.za/english/pdf/Employment.PDF. (consulted Nov. 11, 2006).

Pinch, T., Bijker, W. (1987). The social construction of facts and artefacts. In Bijker, Wiebe, Thomas Hughes, Trevor Pinch, eds., *The social construction of technological systems*. Cambridge, Mass.: MIT Press.

II. PLAY AND SCHOOL ONLINE

M. GRIMES AND ANDREW FEENBERG

RATIONALIZING PLAY

A Critical Theory of Digital Gaming

INTRODUCTION

One of the fastest growing leisure activities of the new century, digital gaming has quickly developed from a marginalized children's pastime into a multi-billion dollar global industry. According to recent estimates by PricewaterhouseCoopers (2008), the global digital games market generated $41.9 billion in sales in 2007, and is expected to surpass $68 billion by 2012 (Bond, 2008). Industry analysis firm comScore estimates that approximately 217 million people worldwide played online games in 2007—a number that continues to multiply as broadband Internet access spreads across the globe (Castronova, 2005). Accordingly, academic attention to digital gaming has increased significantly in recent years as scholars struggle to understand the phenomenon and the booming industry that has formed around it.

Although a number of digital game theories have now emerged from a variety of perspectives, applications of critical theory to the study of digital gaming is still in the preliminary stages. With few exceptions (Kirkpatrick, 2008), existing work in this area (including Postigo, 2003; de Peuter & Dyer-Witheford, 2005; Grimes, 2006) has focused predominantly on the expansion of production processes into digital play (such as labour, commercialization, etc.), reproducing the same work/play binary that has long characterized critical scholarship of play and leisure. Other contributions, such as those of Kline, de Peuter and Dyer-Witheford (2003), Brookey and Booth (2006), and Taylor (2006b, 2006c), which have focused on how the structural limitations of digital games (either commercial, social or technological) impact player agency and interaction, have failed to relate these limitations back to play itself. To date, very little attention has been paid to formulating a critical theory of digital games that would allow a broader understanding of how play practices may themselves come to reproduce the larger processes of rationalization at work within modern capitalist societies.

Yet, there is much to suggest that digital gaming—especially massively multiplayer online games (MMOGs)—is a particularly suitable candidate for a broader application of critical analysis. Games, as Feenberg (1995) argues, "[E]xemplify formally rational systems" (p. 193). Similar to economic markets, legal systems, and scientific research, games break loose from the undifferentiated communicative action of 'ordinary' life to impose a rational form on a sector of experience (Habermas, 1984). Rules define a play domain with unambiguous measures of success and failure and a clear-cut distinction between strategic and non-strategic action. With the addition of technical mediation and commercialism, games become the basis

A. Feenberg and N. Friesen (eds.), (Re)Inventing the Internet: Critical Case Studies, 21–41.

for the production of a form of "institutional order" analyzable on terms similar to those employed in the study of other systems of social rationality (Weber, 1958). As technically mediated, commercial systems through which large populations of players assemble to engage in organized social interaction, MMOGs provide an ideal case study for exploring the relationship between games and social rationality.

The term "social rationality" is used here in a purely descriptive sense to refer to organizational practices that resemble paradigm instances of rationality such as science and mathematics. Three types of practice satisfy this condition: 1) exchange of equivalents; 2) classification and application of rules; and 3) optimization of effort and calculation of results. We do not intend to imply that practices which differ from what we call *social rationality* are irrational, nor do we claim that only science and mathematics are rational in a broad understanding of the term. Practices corresponding to all three principles appear in individual or cultural forms in all societies. For example, a pick-up soccer game has rules but it is not a form of social order imposed by large-scale organization and so does not qualify as an instance of social rationality in our sense. Similarly, a tribal custom sanctioning respect for the property of others or guiding craft work may be rational in the sense of enhancing the survival chances of the community, but if it is not imposed consciously but simply inherited from the past, it too is not socially rational. The *differentia specifica* of social rationality is the role of the three principles of rational practice in social organizations and system media which, on a large scale at least, is unique to modernity.

For the purpose of studying social rationality, Feenberg's (1999) theory of instrumentalization, offers a unique entry point. Instrumentalization theory was introduced to analyze technology on two levels: the primary instrumentalization, which describes how "functions are separated from the continuum of everyday life and subjects positioned to relate to them," and the secondary instrumentalization, which focuses on the social, cultural and political forces that influence design choices as these functions are realized in devices and systems (p. 202). The two instrumentalizations are analytic categories that are helpful in understanding the two-sidedness of technical artifacts, which are both technically rational and socio-culturally meaningful.

Although instrumentalization theory was originally conceived of as a framework for understanding technology, the approach extends to other systems of social rationality as well. As Feenberg (1992) explains, "All rational systems have this double aspect as, on the one hand, a structure of operations based on one or several of the three principles of social rationality, and, on the other hand, as a complex *lifeworld* experienced by those they enrol" (p. 311). As games become rationalized through corporate control and technologization, the rational features fundamental to all formal games assume an unexpected prominence. The exchange of moves between players who are equalized at the outset corresponds to the first principle. Strict rules and strategies exemplify the second and third principle. MMOGs impose these three types of rational practice as follows: players and player moves are standardized through the program code (exchange of equivalents); formal rules are established by the game engine and operators as well as the player community (classification and application of rules); and player efforts are optimized and calculated through numeric levelling and points systems that are further reinforced by the status and social capital granted to players of high standing (optimization of effort and calculation of results).

At the same time, however, MMOGs are constituted by a collaborative play experience that extends beyond these rational systems. Similar to Bakhtin's carnival, MMOGs are characterized by a type of "symbolic action which is rarely mere play: it articulates cultural and political meanings" (Stallybrass & White, 1986, p. 43). MMOG players invest a significant amount of time collaborating to produce cultural content and experiences, as well as transgressing limitations of the game. These players hold a high level of situated knowledge that enables them to engage with digital games technology in unanticipated ways that have tremendous impact on the development, content and function of games within digital culture. Thus, MMOGs can also be understood as a site of struggle between players and corporations over the design and usage of game environments and their contents.

Critical theory offers a unique entry point in this regard, one that integrates and expands upon Marx's critique of capitalism and Weber's critique of rationality. By situating technologies within the social, institutional and ideological contexts from which they are born and within which they evolve, critical theory addresses both the symbiotic relationships that exist between the technical and the social, and the specific threat of technocracy in modern societies. In this way, critical theory allows for a deeper consideration of the ways in which games serve multiple functions for both their owners and players. We propose such an approach through an adaptation of Feenberg's critical theory of technology, applying his concepts of instrumentalization and social rationality to construct an innovative theory of rationalized play as a process of modernity. This "ludification theory" provides a set of criteria for evaluating rationalized games using a two-level approach that considers both the ways in which a game is engaged in types of rational practice, as well as the social, cultural and political conditions within which a game is appropriated and contested by its players.

This paper provides a detailed explanation of ludification theory and the accompanying notion of games as systems of social rationality. The discussion is followed by a case study of *World of Warcraft*, a popular MMOG that currently claims over 12 million players worldwide ("World of Warcraft," 2010) The goal of this chapter is to provide a framework for uncovering the rational properties of MMOGs, and to situate digital games within the larger socio-historical tendency toward rationalization that continues to shape modern play practices. Our intention here is not to argue that rationalized games are qualitatively 'better' or 'worse' than non-rationalized play forms, but rather to initiate debate around the impact and significance of rationalization on the parameters, practices and experience of play.

GAMES AS SYSTEMS OF SOCIAL RATIONALITY

While Romantic notions of "pure play" and "play for play's sake" continue to influence contemporary notions of leisure (Sutton-Smith, 1997), critical theorists have long highlighted the crucial role that play fulfils within advanced capitalism. On the one hand, leisure is integrated to the labour cycle, which requires and organizes periods of rest and recuperation between productive exertions (Marcuse, 1969). On the other hand, the increasing commodification of leisure within mass consumer culture blurs the lines between play and consumption (Bourdieu, 1991). Bourdieu and numerous other theorists argue that the spheres of work and play, if ever they were separate, are now inextricably entangled. This entanglement is primarily viewed in terms of the assimilation of play and leisure into the rational realms of production and consumption, but it is also understood in terms of a spreading infusion of playfulness into the post-industrial work process (de Certeau, 2002). Thus, although play and other leisure forms are often described within play theories as extra-economic, filling a primarily social, spiritual or cognitive function, their actual practice is increasingly understood to occur within a context of complex socio-economic processes.

The relationship between production and leisure remains a key focus within contemporary discussions of the commodification and instrumentalization of play, particularly in recent scholarship on digital multiplayer gaming. For example, the monetization of virtual game economies (which first surfaced in the form of an informal, player-driven exchange of in-game items for real world currency, and has since extended to a variety of sanctioned and unsanctioned revenue models) is often described in labour terms (Grimes, 2006). Taylor describes MMOG players' efforts to inscribe their avatars with personalities, reputations and achievements as a type of labour and collaborative authorship. Others, including Postigo (2003), and Kücklich (2005), have explored how practices such as modding and hacking come to operate as key sources of immaterial labour, oftentimes contributing directly to the digital game development cycle.

As the dominant organizing system of an increasing proportion of our everyday life experience, production easily becomes a prominent focal point in discussions of play and modernity (Gruneau, 1983). For as play activities become more "organized, even administered" (Marcuse, 1965, p. 32), they are increasingly structured by the same values, priorities, skills and norms that drive the workday (Bourdieu, 1991). However, the focus on the relationship between work and play overlooks a key aspect of the rationalization process—namely, that it unfolds differently within different institutional settings (Henricks, 2006). Instead of seeing play as a casualty of economic encroachments, it may be more useful to study how games themselves come to display the same characteristics of rationalization as other institutions of social order and control.

In this respect, games today would be latecomers to modernizing processes that have already incorporated a wide range of generic human behaviours into the rationalization process through technology, markets, and the legal system. Play too now becomes increasingly recontextualized as a foundation of modern society through commodification and technologization. Rationalized play is thus not only congruent with the grand narrative of modernity, but also functions as a social practice that reproduces rationalization within yet another facet of everyday life. Here, we take a cue from Henricks (2006), who argues:

[Play] exhibits social structures only somewhat dissimilar from those found in other parts of life. These structures not only restrict people's personal freedom but also enable them to accomplish things they would be unable to do alone. [...] To play with others is to enter a realm of interconnection that is much more complicated than the play of individuals with the material world. (p. 8–9)

In their non-rationalized form, games do not operate as systems of social rationality—they are not institutionalized on a large scale, and therefore do not generate social order. This changes, however, with the incorporation of games into commerce and technology. The professionalization of sports represents a critical point in the transition from non-rationalized to rationalized games. Standardization in organized sports and gaming clubs goes along with commercialized spectatorship in transforming players and player moves into predictable and measurable units. Gameplay can now be evaluated in terms of the fixed criteria of strict formal rules in order to create a homogenous experience for every participant. That experience can then be commodified in accordance with broadcast rights, audience shares, and the demands of mass consumer culture.

Starting with the professionalization of sporting leagues, technical mediation (in the form of media technology, for example) and social rationalization open a game to the processes of commodification. In some cases a game played by an unpaid community of players might become the recruiting ground for a paid community of professionals performing for an audience of spectators. In others, the products of gameplay may acquire real-world exchange values. In each case, however, the mass commodification of a game will be preceded by its standardization and rationalization.

In spectator sports, however, the control of the conditions of play affects the players far more deeply than the audience. When the division between spectators and players breaks down, as it does in MMOGs, and the rules and boundaries of a game are technically mediated, the participants in the game are incorporated into its design. This significantly reduces the potential for the kind of spontaneous negotiation of rules and exceptions that is possible (and indeed desirable) part of gameplay when a game is played on an individual basis, for instance, between friends on a local playground. Instead, the players' actions in a technically mediated game are reduced to a pre-determined set of possibilities. As games and play are transformed into an increasingly rationalized set of activities involving huge populations for extended periods, they institutionalize a form of social order. The mass of spectator-players is now organized by the technology of the game much as markets organize consumers, state bureaucracies organize citizens and production technology organizes workers.

The transformation of games into sources of social order thus takes place through the incorporation of their rational aspects within both technological and commercial organizational strategies. Gameplay (and the player) becomes structured and rationalized by the game itself, which provides (and oftentimes enforces) the rules to which its players must subscribe. As this form of play is implemented on a wider and wider scale, throughout various types of games and leisure forms, its social significance increases. The players themselves begin to fulfil a crucial role in the game's operation as a large-scale system. Part of what makes these games attractive to other players is their ability to offer a well-developed social dynamic in a shared gameplay experience. In this way, players are transformed into a resource that keeps the game functioning as intended, and legitimizes the exchange value of the game as a 'packaged' social experience. This process is typical of systems of social rationality, wherein even human beings begin to appear as bearers of technical elements available for manipulation by technical organizations.

The essential feature of rationalization is the capture of everyday activities by organizations and media. This includes ordinary play, which has always contained rational qualities (such as rules, points systems, standardized equipment, leagues and associations). Behaviours such as these are present in many other activities as well. They exemplify on a small scale the rational practices of optimizing, exchange of equivalents, and classification and application of rules, but until modern times there were no organizations capable of structuring societies around such behaviours. That transformation occurs when the rational characteristics of everyday practices become the basis of technical, economic, and legal systems and organizations in modern societies. Organizations and media incorporate these characteristics into bureaucratic, commercial, and technical structures that multiply their range and influence.

In this theoretical context, systems of social rationality should be conceived as active agents. Similarly, however, their members can be more or less compliant in fulfilling functions within the structure they lay out. The logic of organizations and media is thus relatively independent of the persons they enrol, but correspondingly, those persons have a certain independence which shows up in actions that induce change, extract plunder, build alternatives surreptitiously in gaps in attention and control, and so on.

Despite the higher levels of rationalization enabled by technical mediation and commercialization, some unpredictable outcomes thus remain not only possible but also likely. No matter how highly rationalized the game, its players remain engaged in a struggle to appropriate and make sense of their play within the contexts of their everyday lives. Not all of their responses conform to the rationalizing intent inscribed in the official modalities of play, and player behaviours can often resist or even challenge the underlying social order. This includes technically specialized interventions, such as hacking and modding, as well as widespread player practices such as cheating, technological appropriations, subversive readings, interpersonal relationships, and the production of unofficial game meta-texts such as fan fiction, walkthroughs, etc. Where these challenges effectively restructure aspects of the game around player demands, we can speak of a *democratic rationalization* in opposition to the rationalization imposed by the official corporate owners.

In many ways, all gameplay ultimately depends on the participation and buy-in of the players, who voluntarily engage in the act of play and, through consensus and collaboration, formulate the parameters, fictions and fantasies of the play experience. No matter how strictly enforced the rules of any game might become, the point of playing a game, as Geertz (1973) argues, is "that it provides a metasocial commentary," a story the players "tell themselves about themselves" (p. 448). While the idea that play is something that is generated by a game's players may at first glance appear at odds with our notion of games as rational systems, we propose that it is within this very tension—between freedom and constraint, between voluntarism and determinism—that play occurs as a form of social practice (Gruneau, 1999), that games come to operate as systems of social order.

FROM RULES TO LUDIFICATION

The rationalization of play draws upon resources that emerge during the transition from informal play activities to organized games. Discussions of this transition appear throughout the foundational scholarship on play, which often distinguishes between play and games. Much of the early work in this area espoused what Sutton-Smith (1997) describes as a "play as progress" ideology, linking the rational features of games (such as formal rules and parameters) to functionalist understandings of play. For example, Huizinga (1955) argues that one of the key features of play is that it "demands order absolute and supreme. The least deviation from it 'spoils the game,' robs it of its character and makes it worthless" (p. 10). Play brings a temporary, limited perfection into the imperfect confusion of everyday life, creating an "exceptional situation" that promotes the formation of social groups and culture.

It is within Caillois' (2001) hierarchical classification of games that we find the clearest articulation (and celebration) of the transition from free play to formal (rule-bound) games, described in terms of a "rank order of progression" that moves along "a continuum between two opposite poles" (p. 13). The first pole, termed paidia, describes forms of play that feature open-ended fantasy and role-play, free-form diversions and unscripted amusements. At the opposite pole, labelled ludus, "this frolicsome and impulsive exuberance is almost entirely absorbed or disciplined by a complementary, and in some respects inverse, tendency…to bind it with arbitrary, imperative, and purposely tedious conventions" (p. 13). Caillois argues that as societies modernize, play is increasingly characterized by ludus, progressing "from turbulence to rules," and given form through the "conventions, techniques and utensils" (p. 29) of rationalized games. As rules and games are institutionalized, he argues, play is transformed "into an instrument of fecund and decisive culture."

However, subsequent theorists have challenged these early idealizations of organized games, rule structures and purposive play. They instead highlight the dialectical relationship that exists between rules and gameplay, "between socially structured possibilities and human agency" (Gruneau, 1999, p. 27). For example, numerous sociologists studying sports and leisure propose that we approach play in terms of its representational function—as a cultural text (e.g. Geertz), as a meta-communicative framework (e.g. Bateson), or in terms of symbolic action or "rhetorics" (e.g. Sutton-Smith). Digital games scholarship has similarly attempted to address the dialectical dimension of gameplay, which is increasingly envisioned as a sort of continuous dialogue that occurs between a game's system (program code, rules, graphical user interface (GUI)) and its players. For instance, Salen and Zimmerman (2004) describe "meaningful play" as emerging "from the relationship between play action and system outcome; it is the process by which a player takes action within the designed system of a game and the system responds to the action" (p. 34).

It is important to remember, however, that within traditional play theories and discussions of games—including those upon which much of the digital games scholarship to date has drawn in conceptualizing emerging forms of "digital play"—gameplay is seen as largely individual or limited to small groupings, and rather marginal to social order. For Caillois and Huizinga, the larger social significance of games lies in the homologies between their structure and social forms, for example, between games of chance and the stock market, or games of skill and career paths. For Geertz and Sutton-Smith, group play provides an important, albeit mostly symbolic, opportunity to re-enact, transgress and otherwise make sense of larger systems of social order (including power relations, social hierarchies, etc.). What is happening today, on the other hand, is rather different.

As described in the previous section, it is not that social order recapitulates certain features of games, but rather that games have themselves become forms of social order. As games become rationalized the rational features fundamental to all formal games assume an unprecedented prominence. Eventually, these games begin to generate their own form of social rationality, imposing all three types of rational practice on millions of players. From this standpoint it becomes clear that the multifaceted institutionalization of games in new processes of social rationalization is the key to the changing dialectics of play.

To explain this state of affairs, we propose that gameplay be understood in terms of a continuum in which the player moves from a general play mood to the specialized state of absorption required for the playing of specific games to, finally, the centralized orchestration of that passage on a mass scale around the technically instituted rules and systems characteristic of rationalized games. In this latter capacity, the theory must take into account the basic rationalizing operations of these games, the power relations and socio-cultural conditions that specify their rules and parameters, and the emergent and subversive play practices that arise from them. Our starting points for developing this theory are Bateson's (1973) reflexive theory of play and Walther's double-aspect theory of the relation between play and games.

Bateson argues that, "Play is paradoxical because it is both within and outside our 'normal' social semantic space" (Walther, 2003). From the everyday, normal standpoint, play has this paradoxical quality insofar as it builds imaginative structures out of ordinary things and situations, and introduces purposeful ambiguity into ordinary actions. As Bateson describes it, play is "a meta-communication that refers exclusively to itself, and not to any external source or receiver." Bateson gives the example of animals pretending to fight. They must actually bite each other and yet do so in such a way as to signify that the bite is not a "real" bite. This special sort of reflexivity is present in everyday playful activities of all sorts and is no doubt the psychic basis on which organized play and games are built. Playfulness in this sense is an identifiable activity but it does not have a definite locus. It is a type of situated or reactive play that is dependent upon the structures and themes provided by what is at the time interpreted to be non-play. Thus within the lifeworld, undifferentiated moments of playfulness occur alongside of and parasitic on the other communicative practices of everyday life, including of course 'serious' activities which in turn become defined as such only when positioned in relation to playfulness.

Walther employs Spencer-Brown's (1969) theory of distinction, as well as Bateson's description of the paradox of play to identify two "transgressions" (we prefer "transformations") that allow the player to enter into the state of mind required for "buy-in" to a game (illustrated as the first and second divisions in Figure 1). The first represents the point at which the player crosses the boundary separating the undifferentiated communicative practices of everyday life from the specialized realm of play. The second occurs when the player moves from a general "play state" into the more focused game state required for effective participation in the action of a particular game in accordance with (or at the very least with an awareness of) its specific rules and criteria. This second transformation is also in line with Caillois' description of the shift from *paidia* to *ludus*.

According to Spencer-Brown, as Walther describes his view, "a universe comes unto being when a space is separated, that is when a distinction is made." In play, this "space" starts out as a purely metaphorical separation of imaginatively conceived spheres, but in the case of games it evolves into a real geographical locale. The "form of the distinction" includes both the differentiated space, which becomes the "marked side" of the space being delineated by the distinction—as well as the remainder, which becomes the "unmarked" side of the distinction.

First, play becomes the "marked" side of the distinction between play and the "unmarked" lifeworld. As the players enter into the play-mood, they adopt a differentiated perspective on play and non-play. For Walther reflexivity enters at this stage, however, we regard the reflexivity of the play-mood as a specific modification of the type of reflexivity that characterizes playfulness in the lifeworld. The difference between that original playfulness and the play-mood is the attempt of the players to give continuity in time and space to their play and the work they engage in to construct an imaginative universe. Once inside the realm of play, all activities which fall outside that universe are reconceptualized as "non-play."

Yet, even while this initial distinction differentiates certain forms of activity from the undifferentiated communicative practices of "non-play," play at this stage remains a highly open and mutable concept, characterized primarily by the boundedness that isolates it from the structures, concerns and consequences of "ordinary" social life. It is this boundedness that allows the player to focus attention on the (play) activities at hand. This changes, however, when play becomes channelled into games and a system of rules is introduced. Walther describes a game as a continuation of the play-mood in that it adopts the praxis of distinction that is established in play, "but its central 'law' is its unique ability to reduce the complexity of play by way of a set of well-defined, non-negotiable rules." This second transformation involves an increase in rationality in the ordinary sense of the term.

Figure 1 (below) represents our adaptation of Walther's model, including the addition of playfulness in the lifeworld at one extreme and, at the other, the technological institution of the rational qualities characteristic of MMOGs and other rationalized games. We have modified Walther's model to illustrate the process of rationalization as comprising three transformations. While the conditions necessary for each of these transformations to occur may manifest as features of the game systems or artifacts, they must first and foremost be understood as shifts in the relationship between the game and its players. All three transformations must occur in order for a game to begin operating as a system of social rationality. In reference to Caillois' term for rational play (*ludus*), as well as the field of ludology, we shall provisionally call this the theory of *ludification*.

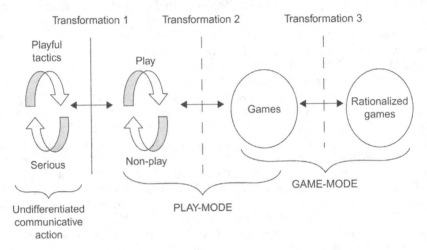

Figure 1. The rationalization of play: a differentiated approach.

The first transformation (illustrated in Figure 1) has been described above as the passage from everyday playfulness, with its momentary and unorganized modification of "serious" contents, to organized play. Play in this sense is not yet constrained by permanent rules and not fully separated from the world of non-play, "reality," which threatens to intrude from time to time. The second transformation is described at length within the play literature. Here, the play-mood becomes rule-governed, and the ambiguity of free play is further reduced under the constraints of the game's fixed temporal and spatial conditions. While still characterized by the play-mood, games are also simultaneously constituted by a game-mood which describes a state of heightened reflexivity involving the player's relationships and interactions with the game's rules and boundaries. This includes the player's desire and attempts to win, to uncover the game's structure and hidden loopholes, to progress or advance through the levels of a game, or to strategize against a competitor. To play a game is thus a dual process, one that demands a delicate balance of playing and gaming. As Walther explains, "One must hold on to the initial distinction (otherwise one is swallowed by the other of play), and one needs constantly to accept the organization, the rule pattern, of the game."

When games are technically mediated and commercialized on a large scale, as in the example of MMOGs or professional sports, they undergo a third transformation into rationalized games. At this stage, the rational properties of reflexivity, boundedness and rule governedness, which are found in all organized games, are intensified to an unprecedented extent. This intensification through technical mediation brings new qualities of precision to the game. The rules and parameters of the game system are programmed into the game code and become ever more tightly enforced and optimized. Play itself becomes subject to increasingly precise forms of measurement and calculation.

Even at this stage, the players possess *initiative* which surfaces in a variety of ways as they engage with and appropriate the technology. The most obvious examples are hacking and modding, but player initiative can manifest in more subtle ways as well. These include the unsanctioned markets for game-items that have cropped up around games such as *EverQuest* and *World of Warcraft*, the collaborative role-playing and community-building that occurs within certain servers or player groups, players' creative appropriations and remixing of game content, and the exchange of game codes and walkthroughs over the Internet. It is here that one discovers the vestiges of non-rationalized play, operating both inside and outside of the formal game structures, occupying the *margin of manoeuver* that co-exists alongside the regimented system of rationalized play.

Much of this activity can be described as playful in our sense of the term. Although the player retains the game-mood necessary to sustain the experiential condition of playing a game, the excessively rigid structures of rationalized games invite a playful response characteristic of the undifferentiated communicative practices of the unmarked lifeworld. In this context, as Sutton-Smith describes, playfulness can be understood as a type of "metaplay" found in activities and attitudes "that play with the normal expectations of play itself," such as "reversal, exaggeration, playing with boundaries, [and] playing with space and time" (p. 147). It is through the unexpected or emergent player activities arising out of playfulness that the unrealized technical potential of digital games is gradually being uncovered.

Referring back to Figure 1, we thus propose that as a game moves toward the right through the intensification of the principles of social rationality, it develops properties that ultimately enable its transformation into a system of social rationality. The process can also operate in the opposite direction, as the activity moves back to a lower level of rationalization, in accordance with a decrease in the presence or intensity of the properties of rationalized games. We have provisionally identified these properties as *reflexivity, boundedness, rule-governedness, precision* and *playfulness* (Table 1). In identifying these properties we are not attempting to define play or to describe games exhaustively. Rather, we propose these properties as key characteristics of the ludification process through which a rationalized game enacts a form of social order.

Table 1. The five properties of ludification

Reflexivity	As play becomes rationalized, it becomes increasingly self-referential and exclusionary of themes and activities from outside the constructed reality of the play activity or game. The system and structures of the game, along with the player's role, gain in primacy at the expense of an increasingly differentiated "outside" or "real" world.
Boundedness	Since play is a differentiated activity, a level of boundedness must always exist in order to distinguish play from the undifferentiated communicative practices of the lifeworld. As games become rationalized, however, the boundaries, in terms of the scope, space and possibilities for play become more limiting, well defined and self-contained.
Rule-Governedness	When play is transformed into a game it becomes governed by a specified set of rules and parameters. As games become rationalized, their rule systems become more rigid and comprehensive as they are determined at the technical and institutional level.
Precision	The specification and standardization of a game's rules is accompanied by an increase in precision, which enables measurement and optimization of the gameplay, in terms of both efforts and results. Like rules, precision leads to a reduction in the scope of what is possible within a game, and transforms play into a quantifiable and predictable set of activities.
Playfulness	Playfulness describes the undifferentiated form of play that occurs within everyday communicative practices. Contrary to the imaginative freedom of play, playfulness is characterized by its situatedness within and dependence upon the game system to provide direction, themes and content. Playfulness can be subversive or reactive, but always functions in direct interaction with the rules, temporality, sequence, and structures of the game.

While all five of these properties must be present for a game to operate as a system of social rationality, each can be established structurally (i.e. by conventions, norms, terms of use contracts, etc.) or technologically in the design of the game system. The following section provides an integrated case study of both ludification (Table 1) and of the rationalization of play (Figure 1), using examples drawn from *World of Warcraft* (WoW), in order to illustrate how we might begin to understand ludification as a process that both enables new forms of social order, as well as creates new opportunities for user resistance and innovation within MMOG gameplay.

CASE STUDY: LUDIFICATION IN *WORLD OF WARCRAFT*

Launched in the US in 2004, WoW remains one of the most popular MMOGs in the history of the genre. Consistently ranked on best-seller lists and often credited for bringing MMOGs into the mainstream, WoW continues to attract widespread public attention. The game currently claims a population of over 10 million players worldwide (Blizzard Entertainment Inc., 2008), generating annual revenues estimated to be in the hundreds of millions (Vella, 2008). Among digital games scholars, academic interest in WoW is accordingly quite high, and over the past two years a large amount of MMOG research has focused on the game and its population, design and cultural impact. This research has produced numerous chapters (e.g. Taylor, 2006b; Humphreys, 2008), a special issue of *Games and Culture* journal (Krzywinska & Lowood, 2006), and at least one edited collection (Corneliussen & Rettberg, 2008).

While much has now been written about WoW players—in terms of their cultural practices, communities, social interactions and in-game behaviours—less attention has been paid to the game's underlying technological, social and political structures. Yet more recent studies of MMOGs, and of WoW in particular, indicate that there is a clear need for sustained research in this area. As Taylor writes, "Rather than simply identifying 'emergent culture' as a prime property of MMOG life and stopping there, we also need a better understanding of the complex nature of player-produced culture and its relation to the technical game artifacts" as well as an "understanding the role systems of stratification and forms of social control play in these game worlds" (p. 319). Thus, while our use of WoW as a case study builds upon a relatively broad corpus of research, our focus on the game's role as a system of social rationality represents an important departure.

Reflexivity

Like other digital games, WoW displays and invites a high level of reflexivity through the very nature of its interactive design. As Kirkpatrick (2008) notes,

> In computer games critical engagement with the interface and the computer as a machine with comprehensible, technical rules of behaviour is the norm. [...] Games use technical knowledge and understanding of computer behaviour to work out when a solution applied to one game will probably work for another. (p. 128)

This occurs regardless of the specific aesthetic and narrative context of the game. In order to participate in WoW, the player must learn to manoeuver in the game environment, discover the game control keys (which keys to press and when), develop some sense of the game's mechanics and the range of possible actions (at least at an introductory level), and figure out the levelling system and in-game currency. As the underlying structures of the game are revealed, the players' reflexive engagement becomes increasingly sophisticated, involving activities such as fine tuning certain skills instead of others in order to construct a specific type of character, or rearranging the hot key set-up to increase playability.

Reflexivity is heightened when the player experiences tension vis-à-vis the rules and technical features of the game. Examples include those early stages of gameplay when a player is first learning the rules, or when players are unable to make a desired action (such as attempting to climb an unclimbable cliffside), or when heavy traffic forces players to wait before they can connect with a server. In the absence of such tensions, the restrictive and rationalizing qualities of the game's design are experienced primarily as feedback in a cycle of interactivity, much as interactions in the "real" world are experienced as both constrained and enabled by physical laws. As Rehak (2003) argues, these interactions are themselves a pleasurable aspect of digital gaming, since "part of what users seek from computers is continual response to their own actions—a reflection of personal agency made available onscreen as surplus pleasure" (p. 111).

The points and levelling systems assigned to player actions and game objects also extend reflexivity by drawing the player's attention to the game's underlying numerical structures. Like other digital games, WoW has a pre-determined and highly specified levelling system that quantifies player actions and achievements (such as completing "Quests," clearing an "Instance Dungeon," or defeating your opponents on a "player-versus-player" (PvP) Battleground) by assigning them a value expressed in "Experience Points" (XP). All players start at level 1 (unless they have purchased a pre-levelled character) and must accrue a sufficient amount of XP before advancing to the next level, a system that is reproduced (with each level requiring greater amounts of XP to complete) until the player reaches level 70 (the current level cap which will soon be raised to 80). In addition, each character's specific attributes, such as strength, stamina and intellect, are expressed numerically, as are health and mana (the energy used for casting spells), which require constant replenishment. Meanwhile, the majority of in-game items, even Quest items, have an exchange value. Items (and even full characters) can be bought and sold for Gold (the WoW currency) or exchanged in a variety of ways, both through the game system and through unsanctioned trade on the "real-world" market.

The game's numerical systems constantly communicate to the player, Stallabrass (1996) argues, an unambiguous "idea of progress [that] is always present in the game, shadowing and interpreting the action" (p. 90). While players are always free to ignore the game's numerical structures, there are many rewards and benefits associated with "levelling up." With each new level attained, the player also gains access to new (increasingly challenging and intricate) quests, items, abilities and areas of the game world. The high visibility of the XP system and the privileging of progress within WoW provides players with a clearly articulated template for "proper" (if not mandatory) gameplay, one which reveals and highlights the very measurement criteria upon which the player's action are evaluated.

Boundedness

While the game environment of WoW is expansive, collaborative, open-ended and continuously evolving, it is also bounded by its design and program code. The game code provides the scope and limitations for the vast majority of in-game activities—it makes up the game's environment, supplies it with laws of physics, determines the range of actions that are possible (walk, run, sit, attack, cast a spell), for whom (e.g. only Paladins can use a "Divine Shield" spell) and at what frequency (e.g. Hearthstones that teleport the player to a pre-selected 'home base' can't be used more than once an hour). Within WoW, the scope of what is and is not possible—in terms of player actions and interactions with the virtual environment—is not only discovered in the act of playing (as in non-rationalized games) but is technically enforced by the game engine. In manoeuvring through a digital game, players interact with the database through a parser, which reads player actions as a series of "if-then" commands (Kirkpatrick, 2004). At the level of human-computer interaction, gameplay is thus reducible to a series of variables, selections drawn from an immense but nonetheless finite number of possible options, expressed in the rudimentary language of computer code.

Moves and choices that have not been encoded into the game program or otherwise afforded by the design (whether intentionally or not) are simply impossible except through technically specialized interactions such as hacking or modding. In the case of WoW, which was specifically built to enable high levels of player agency and independence, even technical intervention is to some extent allowed by design. As Taylor (2006a) describes, the WoW game system was constructed with a flexible user-interface, intended to allow "player-developers" to make modifications that "are not simply cosmetic but can provide core functionality to the game, even altering the nature of play itself" (p. 326). In any case, since the majority of players do not have the technical expertise required to intervene at this level most player actions fall firmly within the scope of what is provided by the Blizzard game engine.

This does not mean that every possible move or outcome has been imagined or predetermined by the game's designers. Players engage in a variety of unanticipated and even unsanctioned behaviours, from cheating and "gold-farming" to buying and selling characters on the real-world market (Castronova, 2005). Players appropriate the game environment for a variety of social and creative purposes, from initiating and maintaining personal relationships, to using the game as a staging ground for the production of machinima. Past research has also identified numerous examples of "emergent play" within WoW, including a number of incidents involving large numbers of players staging a collaborative protest by gathering together at a specific time and place in order to overload (and therefore crash) a server and communicate a point to Blizzard and to other players (Taylor, 2006c).

The game also contains occasional glitches and produces unintended outcomes, which add to the game's "emergent" qualities. In 2007, for example, WoW was struck by an unplanned "pandemic" that emerged unexpectedly out of a spell intended to spread an infectious disease among a contained group of advanced-level players, within the specific context of an instance dungeon "boss battle" (the last monster of a level or quest, usually by far the most challenging). Over 4 million players were infected during the course of the "Corrupted Blood" pandemic, causing the kind of "social chaos that comes from a large-scale outbreak of a deadly disease" (Lofgren & Fefferman, 2007, p. 625). It is important to remember, however, that these types of events do nonetheless occur within a pre-established realm of possibility, bounded by the game's technological affordances—even though some of these affordances may not yet have been discovered by either the players or the game's designers before they erupt.

Another way in which WoW exhibits properties of boundedness is through its narrative and aesthetic features. Through a combination of rich graphics, sound architecture, and spatiality, WoW provides players with an extremely detailed and coherent *gameworld.* As computer animation techniques, 3D modeling technologies and sound engineering in digital games become more sophisticated and intricate, the game's space and artificial environments are not only increasingly predetermined but also increasingly immersive, constructing a distinctly bounded playspace, the limits of which are reinforced by the internal logic of the game. The affordances and limitations of the source code are thus not merely perceived as establishing permitted gameplay, but also as constituting the 'physical' reality of the gameworld.

The naturalization of the game's design and parameters is facilitated by the graphical user interface (GUI), which prevents most players from engaging directly with the infinite potential of the "game as code" (Kirkpatrick, 2004). The player is isolated from the code, which is the underlying object of her/his actions. The control system, or "interface between player and operating system" (Stallabrass 1996, p. 96), translates the player's desired actions to the parser 'behind the screen.' As a player learns the design and parameters of the source code, they become internalized as part of the 'physical' reality of the gameworld. These parameters, in conjunction with the norms and conventions created by the player community, come to define what the game is, as well as what it is not.

Rule-Governedness

These first two properties of ludification (reflexivity and boundedness) are intertwined with the third property, rule-governedness. As described above, unlike the rule systems of non-rationalized games, technologically mediated rules are rigid and precise, and cannot be negotiated or challenged by the average, non-specialist player. In WoW, many of the game rules and parameters are established, maintained and communicated by the game's database, and hence integrated into the technological design of the game itself. The 'laws' of this system can thus be enforced quite explicitly, embedded within the very fabric of the gamespace (including its aesthetic, spatial and environmental dimensions) and game design. Within WoW, however, technological mediation is just one of the ways that rules and community norms come to structure gameplay and player behaviour; it operates in conjunction with formal and informal systems of surveillance, corporate law, group norms and player expectations.

As is common practice among commercial MMOG operators, Blizzard requires WoW players to agree to an end-user license agreement (EULA) and terms of use (TOU) contract before entering into the game. Player activities and in-game communications are then monitored, both by the game's automated systems and by Blizzard employees, to ensure continued compliance. In addition to making compliance to the game's official "rules of conduct" a condition of service (meaning that a player's account can be frozen or deleted if they disobey), these contracts demand that players waive a number of their rights while inside the game environment, including rights to freedom of speech, moral rights and authorship rights. In this way, Herman et al (2006) argue, WoW establishes its own "forms of governance and moral economies of practice" (p. 191) to which players must submit or risk expulsion. Furthermore, many of the terms outlined within the EULA and TOS seek to enlist players in legal relationships that extend well beyond the confines of the game. A key example of this is the sweeping intellectual property terms included in the EULA, which claim exclusive ownership rights over anything that players say or do while inside the game environment.

Within WoW, rules are also institutionalized at the social level by community norms and expectations. A large part of what makes playing an online game enjoyable is its ability to offer a well-developed social dynamic, and part of this involves the construction and negotiation of social norms. Some informal rules of play are derived out of the game's narrative and genre conventions (e.g. every character is either a member of the Alliance or part of the Horde, each of which comes with its own history and expectations), while others might stem from the "code of conduct" of an especially popular or high-profile Guild (groups of players that are formalized within the game design). Some emerge from the consensus of the larger player community, while others represent the perspectives and interpretations of a small number of particularly vocal players. At times community norms come to operate as systems of social control that work to discipline, exclude or otherwise classify players and behaviours. For example, Taylor's (2006b) recent ethnographic study of WoW uncovered numerous examples of Guilds setting minimum age requirements, formally excluding players under the age of 18 years.

Precision

As described above, within WoW, gameplay is optimized and calculated through leveling systems and capitalist-based virtual economies that serve to measure the player's activities and evaluate the player's actions and progress. On one level, WoW's leveling systems draw upon conventions established within the tradition of table-top role-playing games (such as "Dungeons and Dragons"), which use a special set of dice to determine the outcome of events and player actions. However, these systems are also byproducts of digitization, which enables hitherto unimaginable levels of precision in the measurement, recording and analysis of the online activities of any number of players. Digitization not only allows game rules and structures to become immutable virtual realities, it also transforms player actions, in-game communications and creative contributions into neatly standardized and easily retrievable data. This enables an ongoing and fairly detailed surveillance of player activities and interactions.

Precise knowledge of individual players' greatly facilitates the regulation of player behaviour, as well as the enforcement of rules and other "terms of use." But more importantly, once players' in-game communications, contributions and activities have been digitized and recorded, the data can then sorted, mined and made sense of for a variety of commercial purposes. Digitization, Mosco (2004) argues, "[E]xpands the commodification of content by extending opportunities to measure and monitor, package and repackage entertainment and information" (p. 156). Game designers use intricate tracking and data mining systems to discover new patterns in behaviour and player preferences, which can then be used to ameliorate or expand the game design (through patches or expansion sets). They can also compile the data in various forms to create highly detailed user trend reports, which can then be sold to external parties to be used in advertising campaigns or other marketing initiatives.

The principle of precision spills over into player practices as well. Not only do players experience the precise measurement of their own powers and status by the game as described above, they also participate in measuring, A recent example, described by Taylor (2006b), is the growing use of mod interventions that enable a precise evaluation of player actions by other players. These player-produced mods not only facilitate a growing "focus on quantification" (p. 332) among the players who use them, but also enable players to engage in new forms of social coercion, evaluating each others' performance through the seemingly objective lens of the measurement tools. As Taylor writes, "through their rationalization and quantification of action, they also strongly inform (and potentially limit) what is seen as "good play" or what is viewed as reasonable" (p. 332).

Playfulness

The final property, playfulness, describes the players' relationship to and negotiation with the social rationality of the game. Source codes and databases establish what actions are possible within the WoW game environment, which greatly reduces opportunities for imaginative freedom. At the same time, the reflexive properties of the game invite the player to engage in self-referential forms of activity, such as discovering the limits and affordances of the game design. Because playfulness consists of a structurally embedded and reactive form of play, it occurs in dialogue with the game's underlying structures, playing with and occasionally against the system. This shift in the focus and contents of player activities is a key factor in the unanticipated gameplay (including player appropriation, subversion and innovation) that continues to unfold within even highly structured and rationalized games. Playfulness brings about a higher level of initiative vis-à-vis the digital game system.

Through playfulness, the player contributes to, subverts, and reinterprets the rules and laws imposed by the technical system. In each of the previous sections (reflexivity, boundedness, rule-governedness and precision), many of the player practices we described are also examples of playfulness. These range from basic trial and error explorations of the game mechanics, to the transgressive actions of players who aggravated the "Corrupted Blood" pandemic by purposefully spreading infection, to the development of mods that uncover the underlying numerical logic of player actions.

The subversive potential of playfulness is obvious in game hacking and modding, but it also surfaces in quotidian player practices, from the collaborative development of social norms to the practice of coordinating a server crash as a form of protest. Playfulness can contribute to the technological design of digital games in unforeseen ways. Of course, player initiative can also be met with resistance—from other players, if the activity interferes with their own play, or from the game's designers, if the activity interferes with design objectives or corporate priorities. But undirected and unexpected player initiatives can uncover the unrealized technical potential of digital game technologies. It is here that democratic rationalization of this technological form becomes possible.

CONCLUSION

Whereas the political, cultural, economic and technological features of MMOGs are all subject to ongoing attention and analysis within games studies, the literature to date has so far failed to adequately relate these processes to the widespread rationalization of play, leisure and the lifeworld as a whole. We have sought to remedy this oversight by positioning games as systems of social rationality operating within the larger socio-historical context of modernity, and by providing a framework (ludification) for a more comprehensive exploration of the processes through which game rules become technically mediated, play practices become institutionalized, and players become rationalized (and professionalized or com-modified). Furthermore, a more comprehensive understanding of contemporary shifts in the role and function of play as it becomes a rationalizing process of modernity, provides a unique entry point for discussions about the commo-dification and technical mediation of leisure that transcends the outdated work/play binary that informs so much of the literature to date.

In proposing that games can operate as systems of social rationality, we have attempted to construct a theory of play that takes into account the changing nature and function of games within contemporary capitalist societies. We have identified five properties of ludification, which explain how games, arising out of undifferen-tiated communicative practices, gradually evolve into an increasingly rationalized form of activity (Figure 1). The ludification theory shows how essential properties of games lend themselves to appropriation and transformation into systems of social rationality. The theory explains how play comes to operate as a source of institutional order, enacting the same principles found within other more commonly recognized rationalizing processes such as technologization, bureaucratization and commodification.

As seen in the case of WoW, technical mediation opens games up to further processes of rationalization, such as commodification. The congruence between various rationalized systems is a key component in understanding how play fits in with the larger project of modernity. In each case the technologization of the game invests properties identified in the ludification theory with new meaning as structures of social rationality. Due to recent developments within the realm of MMOGs, including the debates around the legality of EULAs and growing public concern about corporate usage of digitized personal information, an approach that considers how rationalization in one area of social life leads to increased compatibility with other rationalized spheres seems particularly timely and necessary.

To this end, we have proposed ludification theory as the basis for a critical study of rationalized play forms that includes but is certainly not limited to *World of Warcraft*. Future work in this area should focus not only on extending its application to other MMOGs, but to other forms of technically mediated multiplayer games as well. Of equal importance is the continued exploration of the property of playfulness, as well as the opportunities for democratic rationalization within all systems of social rationality. Ultimately, the study of games must always be aware of the fact that online digital play is much more than a technological divertissement. It also forms virtual communities in which rational systems of commerce, technology, and gameplay interact to produce a multilayered social experience.

REFERENCES

Bateson, G. (1973). *Steps to an ecology of mind*. New York: Ballantine Books.

Bond. P. (2008, June 18). Video game sales on winning streak, study projects. *Hollywood Reporter*.

Bourdieu, P. (1991). Sport and social-class. In C. Mukerji M. Schudson (Eds.), *Rethinking popular culture: contemporary perspectives in cultural studies*. Berkeley: University of California Press.

Caillois, R. (2001). *Man, play and games*. Chicago: University of Illinois Press.

Castronova, E. (2005). *Synthetic worlds: The business and culture of online games*. Chicago: The University of Chicago Press.

Corneliussen, H.G., & Walker Rettberg, J. (Eds.) (2008). *Digital culture, play, and identity: A* World of Warcraft *reader*. Cambridge: The MIT Press.

de Certeau, M. (1984). *The practice of everyday life*. Los Angeles: University of California Press.

de Peuter, G., & Dyer-Witheford, N. (2005). A playful multitude? Mobilising and counter-mobilising immaterial game labour. *Fibreculture* (5).

Feenberg, A. (1992). Subversive rationalization: technology, power and democracy. *Inquiry 35*(3–4), 301–322.

Feenberg, A. (1995). *Alternative modernity: The technical turn in philosophy and social theory*. Los Angeles: University of California Press.

Feenberg, A. (1999). *Questioning technology*. New York: Routledge.

Grimes, S.M. (2006). Online multiplayer games: A virtual space for intellectual property debates? *New Media & Society 8*(6), 969–990.

Habermas, J. (1984). *The theory of communicative action: lifeworld and system: a critique of functionalist reason* (trans. T. McCarthy). Boston: Beacon Press.

Huizinga, J. (1950/1955). *Homo ludens: A study of the play element in culture*. Boston: Beacon Press.

Humphreys, S. (2008). Ruling the virtual world. *European Journal of Cultural Studies 11*(2), 149–171.

Kirkpatrick, G. (2004). *Critical technology: A social theory of personal computing*. Burlington, VT: Ashgate Publishing Company.

Kirkpatrick, G. (2008). *Technology and social power*. New York: Palgrave Macmillan Ltd.

Krzywinska, T., & Lowood, H. (2006). Guest editors' introduction. *Games and Culture 1*(4), 279–280.

Kücklich, J. (2005). Precarious playbour: modders and the digital games industry. *Fibreculture* (5).

Lofgren, E.T., & Fefferman, N.H. (2007). The untapped potential of virtual game worlds to shed light on real world epidemics. *The Lancet Infectious Diseases 7*(9), 625–629.

Marcuse, H. (1969). *An essay on liberation*. Boston, MA: Beacon Press.

Mosco, V. (2004). *The digital sublime: Myth, power, and cyberspace*. Cambridge: The MIT Press.

Postigo, J. (2003). From Pong to Planet Quake: post-industrial transitions from leisure to work. *Information, Communication & Society 6*(4), 593–607.

Spencer-Brown, G. (1969). *Laws of form*. London: George Allen & Unwin Ltd.

Stallabrass, J. (1996). *Gargantua: Manufactured mass culture*. New York: Verso.

Sutton-Smith, B. (1997). *The ambiguity of play*. Cambridge: Harvard University Press.

Taylor, T.L. (2006a). *Play between worlds: Exploring online game culture*. Cambridge: The MIT Press.

Taylor, T.L. (2006b). Does WoW change everything?: How a PvP server, multinational player base, and surveillance mod scene caused me pause. *Games and Culture 1*(4), 318–337.

Taylor, T.L. (2006c). Beyond management: Considering participatory design and governance in player culture. *First Monday 11*(9).

Vella, M. (2008). Inside the world of Blizzard. *Business Week Online*, August 20. Retrieved Sept. 18 2008 from http://www.businessweek.com/innovate/content/aug2008/id20080820_123140.htm

Walther, B.K. (2003). Playing and gaming: Reflections and classifications. *Games Studies: The International Journal of Computer Game Research 3*(1).

Weber, M. (1958). *The protestant ethics and the spirit of capitalism*, (trans. T. Parsons). New York: Scribners.

World of Warcraft subscriber base reaches 12 million worldwide (2010, Oct 7). *Press Release*, Irvine, CA: Blizzard Entertaiment Inc.

EDWARD HAMILTON AND ANDREW FEENBERG

ALTERNATIVE RATIONALISATIONS AND AMBIVALENT FUTURES

A Critical History of Online Education

THE QUESTION OF EDUCATIONAL TECHNOLOGY

What is the significance of the Internet for higher education? This question – the central concern of a vast, diverse and growing body of research and development spanning three decades – remains, despite the intense activity surrounding it, something of an enigma. Educators, enthusiastic about the promise of new technologies, have focused on testing and exploring the pedagogical utility of new tools and systems. Administrators, responding to an austere operating climate, have envisaged virtual classrooms as a means of expanding the reach and enhancing the revenue streams of their institutions. Corporate developers have seen the Internet (well, really the Web and now Web 2.0) as a means of appealing to student "consumers," gaining entry into the multi-billion dollar education market, and transforming education into a profitable industry. Those wary of the high flown rhetoric of a technological revolution have looked askance at online education as, at best, a cheapening of the liberal humanist traditions of higher learning and at worst an instrument of economic rationalisation in the university.

Regardless of what sector the question comes from, or of what concerns are embraced by the various answers that have been generated for it, all are united in one feature – a forgetfulness of the *history* of online education. Popular and scholarly commentators have, in addressing the key question of technology and education, failed to note that any significance new technologies might have for social processes will be relative to a course of development over time and in relation to the whole set of concerns and priorities shaping those processes. This course of development is not linear nor is it driven by technology alone. Rather it is fractal and shaped through interactions between specific social interests and the material possibilities that are opened to social practices by technical systems.

In what follows we address a portion of this deep and complex history. Beginning from conflicts arising in the late 1990s over the meaning of online education for the future of the university, we explore how these conflicts arose relative to a particular model of computer-mediated education that dates back at least to the 1960s, and whose spirit is much older than that. Revealing this history is, however, only part of the story. If conflicts over the meaning of online education are relative to a model for its development, then different models might suggest different developmental trajectories and supply a different ground for a critical politics of technology in the contemporary university. To demonstrate this,

A. Feenberg and N. Friesen (eds.), (Re)Inventing the Internet: Critical Case Studies, 43–70.

we introduce the case of an early experiment in educational computer conferencing at the Western Behavioral Sciences Institute. This experiment – in essence the first fully online education program – generated not just a unique use of technology in education, but a different developmental model for online education, revealing the latter as subject to multiple determinations along fundamentally different lines. In the conclusion we consider the implications of our historicisation of online education for concrete developments in the field. While addressing the historical dimension of online education cannot resolve the enigma of its meaning or value, it may serve to clarify certain lines of development and their implications for policy and practice.

A DETERMINISTIC POLITICS OF ONLINE EDUCATION

Online education was invented by academics, and at its origins it reflected their concerns, values and pedagogical conceptions. But they lacked the resources necessary to implement their innovation on a wide scale. University computer centres were often uncooperative, administrators indifferent, and business prospects as yet unimagined. Individual faculty might gain support for small experiments, but in its early days online education seemed more a hobby of a few odd champions than a significant advance.

All this changed in the mid-1990s, when corporate CEOs, futurists, state bureaucrats and their sinister lieutenants in university administrations, riding on the rising tide of revolutionary furore surrounding the Internet, began to see technology as a solution to mounting and cumulative crises in higher education. In the confluence of seemingly insoluble budgetary difficulties, word of a coming boom in student numbers, and demands from government and industry for a highly educated workforce, online education was being called upon to solve some of the deepest economic, pedagogical and organisational problems of the university. In solving these problems, however, online education was also expected to transform higher education in a way that would leave no corner of its institutions untouched.

Computer and software companies saw a market in this transformation and suddenly online education was on everyone's lips as the Next Big Thing. Those who had worked quietly in the field for the previous fifteen years were ignored in the rush to a technological revolution that, it became rapidly clear, was all about money – money to be saved by substituting capital for labour on campus along lines familiar from many earlier deskillings of crafts and professions – with only secondary consideration given to the pedagogical and professional concerns that had driven early innovation.

Online education thus emerged in the mid-1990s as an object of considerable political contention in the university. It became embedded in a rhetoric of reform which set traditional structures and practices in opposition to the next evolutionary stage in higher education. The "virtual university" stood as a technological destiny, a logical replacement for the cumbersome and anachronistic "traditional" institution. In such evangelical discourses, online education was represented as an inevitable challenge and transformative force. In the stronger version of this rhetoric, brick-

and-mortar universities would vanish – no doubt in a puff of pipe smoke and a rustle of tweeds – to be replaced by the effervescent movement of digital information in global telecommunications networks. The structural transformation of academic labour and the academic profession was depicted as a both necessary prerequisite for and an inevitable consequence of the increasing technological mediation of higher education.

The zeal with which this evangelical vision was professed is perhaps difficult to remember in a more sober age.[1] Nevertheless, it was not so very many years ago that encomiums on the "death of the traditional university" were being uttered with little caution by university administrators, marketers, journalists, futurologists, the heads of research organisations, government officials, and even some faculty. Peter Drucker's (1997) prediction that traditional universities would become "wastelands" in the early decades of the twenty-first century was only an inflated version of a claim being made in calmer tones elsewhere (Lenzner & Johnson, 1997). According to some, the virtualisation of the university would mean the replacement of "physical process with new processes that can be accomplished over networks" (Katz & Oblinger, 2000:2). For others, the technology heralded the "unbundling of higher education services" with "different providers carrying out different functions: curricular development, delivery of instructional modules, provision of student services, student evaluation, and awarding credentials" (Wallhaus, 2000: 22). The intensified division of labour made possible by breaking the faculty's monopoly on education would demote professors to deprofessionalised "content experts," or at least allow universities to "rationalise" their labour practices. One university professor, commenting on and offering admonishment to faculty resistant to technological change, stated that

> Universities are in the information business, and the information railroad is coming…we would be wise to ask whether the particularly quaint way that we manufacture, distribute and deliver education will survive the arrival of the information railroad. (Wulf, 1998: 1–2)

It is this type of rhetoric that critics of online education responded to and came to equate with the developmental trajectories of the field despite the wide variety of actual practice. For critics, the dissolution of the university into digital networks would make possible the further dissolution of the traditional social and professional structures in which higher education had been embedded for close to a millennium. Thus, online education became a major focus of debate over the future of higher education. The debate, however, was one in which the question of online education as an actually existing socio-technical movement with a complex history became inseparable from the evangelical rhetoric surrounding its underlying technologies. Once "online education" had been solidified as a discursive figure, the debate could be carried out with little detailed examination of developments in the field. Its "nature" was fixed, and conflicting interests polarised around it.

Online education thus appears in one of two registers in discussions of the role of technology in university reform in the late 1990s. One side presents a story of the progressive development of technology as it is applied to the organisation of higher education, leading to pedagogical advances and to the new forms of administration required for the realisation of the technology's full potentials, both pedagogical and economic. Peter Drucker's famous claim, quoted above, is a much-cited, if extreme, instance of this view.[2] Here, online education is understood as a concatenation of tools that impose certain adaptations and structural adjustments. The alignment of these changes with particular social interests is regarded as merely coincidental.[3] Online education is neutralised to the point where any suggestion of a political context or historical foundation disappears behind a façade of technological inevitability.

The other side presents a socio-political account of the dynamics of corporate power in the university. Online education is seen here as a lever of neoliberal reform, an extension to the university of a capitalism that is now digital, global, and knowledge-based. Information technology has supplied capital with a powerful means of integrating and transforming a site of social practice previously independent of markets and direct economic production. In David Noble's words, "...here as elsewhere technology is but a vehicle and a disarming disguise" (Noble, 2002: 26).[4] In this view, online education is reified around political-economic interests that it is claimed unequivocally to represent. Commodification, commercialisation, and marketisation are understood as fundamental dimensions of the technology and its consequences for higher education and the university.

Both sides of the debate pay particular attention to the way in which technology will, for better or worse, transform the professional structure and pedagogical practices of university teaching. The problem with these accounts is not that their claims, taken individually, are entirely incorrect, nor that they point to insignificant trends in the university. The problem lies in the general philosophical orientation to technology underlying *both* versions of the story. On each side technology emerges as a *fait accompli* with which the university must comply or which it must reject out of hand in defence of traditional academic values and priorities. Both views are based on essentially deterministic assumptions, drawing on a perspective that has been rigorously criticised in both philosophical and empirical study of technology.[5]

This has led to an unfortunate situation in which each account, while sharing an identical spontaneous philosophy of technology, appears exclusive of the other, divided between priorities and values that are imagined to be irreconcilable. To accept online education means to accept a logic of neoliberal rationalisation, and to defend the traditional university seems only to mean opposition to technology. While some research has noted and responded to this dilemma,[6] the situation in the late 1990s was such that "online education" was constructed in these polarised and reifying terms.

This impasse is in need of redressing from within an alternative philosophical orientation that can widen the scope of critical engagement with online education. At stake here is not only the viability of a critical position, but a real historical possibility – that the critique of online education could supply a developmental basis for online education rather than being merely a knee-jerk reaction against technology. Critical theory of technology supplies such an orientation in its emphasis on the historical and political dynamics of technological change.[7] In order to resituate technology in the politics of the contemporary university, we will present two cases in the history of educational computing – the development of CAI against a background of theoretical, pedagogical and organisational concerns of distance education in the 1960s & 1970s, and an early experiment in educational computer conferencing in the 1980s. We argue that in these two cases (and others like them) can be discerned two competing paths of development for online education – paths whose realisations offer different stakes in the politics of university reform in the present. In the final section of this chapter, we will draw some conclusions from these cases regarding theory, methodology, policy and development in online education.

COMPUTERISATION AND COMMODIFICATION – THE CASE OF CAI

Critical observers of new media in higher education have envisaged these technologies in terms of the commodification of knowledge, the commercialisation of education, the automation of instruction and the subordination of education to economic ends. In a paradigmatic statement of this critique, Lyotard (1979) sees the computer as reducing knowledge to "quantities of information" and "rigorously [externalising knowledge] with respect to the knower" (Lyotard, 1979: 13). Aronowitz (1999) concurs: in computer-mediated education the student "responds to packaged material," which is prepared by star academics but delivered by a casualised labour force. In Werry's (1999) account, this labour force is replaced by actors, presumably because once the content is supplied its delivery is best handled by the real experts in performance. Noble (2002), too, follows this line, linking online education to the commodified educational products and Taylorised labour process of early 20th century correspondence schools. The critics agree: computer mediation means a reduction of education to information delivery, of faculty to deprofessionalised "content providers," and of the university to a site of commodity production.

As strong as such critiques seem, the empirical and historical reality of educational computing is a great deal more complex than the critics' work suggests. Critics tend to focus on a narrow slice of the spectrum of educational computing and online education, and to argue from a narrow set of historical precedents for the processes they believe themselves to be observing.

In fact, similar critiques have appeared throughout the history of educational technologies and media, from Plato's critique of writing in the *Phaedrus*, to fears in the 1950s that television would usher in the era of the automatic student and the robot professor (Plato, 1973; Smith, 1958). What Plato had to say about writing is not much different from later critiques of educational computing, centring as he does on the way in which the medium offers a static embodiment of knowledge and a vehicle for its distribution independent of social relations. Plato was clearly thinking of educational computing when he prophesied that "pupils will receive a quantity of information without proper instruction," which requires dynamic contexts of co-presence (Plato, 1976: 96). As more recent critics approached the computer, so Plato approaches writing as a means of "externalising knowledge from the knower." Such critiques are rooted in a formal conception of how media act on information – the technologies are conceived as essentially *representational* in nature, and it is as such that they are understood to relate to education according to a narrow pedagogy of information delivery and acquisition.[8]

Are critical appraisals reacting to some essential quality in the media that are their objects? If so, then the vision of technology-mediated education they produce is a destiny and we have little choice but to fall in line or rise up in resistance to technology. But while the critique of commodification via computing seems prescient today, Plato's formally similar critique of alphabetic writing seems preposterous – who today would take a line against writing in favour of a return to purely oral scholarship? And yet these qualities of the technology appeared real and palpable to the Philosopher, as the qualities of new technologies do to critics today. The answer to this dilemma lies in shifting our view of the relation of these qualities to the technologies that apparently embody them. If we see these technical qualities not as essences but as *potentials* that must be activated in line with certain conceptions of education and certain features of its development contexts, a different history and a different critique reveals itself. A bit of historical background will help to clarify the point.

The history of online education begins with the appropriation of the computer as a pedagogical tool in the 1960s and 1970s in the field of distance education. This appropriation produced a model of computer-mediated education that both informed critical understandings of the meaning and value of the computer in higher learning and that came to be imported into later critiques of online education. That model was Computer Assisted Instruction (CAI).

CAI was an early form of computer-mediated education in which learning materials were programmed into mainframes, and structured through interactive features whereby students could review, practice and be tested on a given content. Students accessed the system remotely by dial-up connection from dumb terminals (Alessi & Trollip, 1985). Their progress was managed by the system itself through pre-programmed tests and feedback mechanisms. While communication functions were eventually added, they were conceived to facilitate content delivery and monitoring functions, amounting to little more than quality control apparatuses.[9]

The first CAI system was the perhaps ironically-named PLATO (Rahmlow et al., 1980).[10] From the beginning, "the goal of PLATO was to deliver cost-effective computer-assisted instruction" (Kinzer et al., 1986: 26) – a goal which was supported technically by the centralisation of standardised instructional resources, and by increases in central processing power to handle large numbers of simultaneous users (Woolley, 1994). Like other CAI systems, PLATO was designed to run on mainframes – thus programming capabilities and information storage remained concentrated in the central host even after it became technically possible to distribute greater interactivity and control to remote users with the development of PCs and packet switching (Pagliaro, 1983; Rahmlow et al., 1980). Cost-effectiveness and control over both information processing operations and course information were posited as twin variables in PLATO's development. By the mid-1970s, it appeared as if the general goal of the system was being realised – single installations could simultaneously handle around one-thousand users and were in operation for a range of courses worldwide. The sharing of resources between facilities meant that PLATO courses could be delivered to an expanding audience (Darack, 1977; Woolley, 1994).

The goal of cost-effectiveness was also supported in the system's organisation of course design and delivery. PLATO's basic principle was to leverage the computer's information storage, analysis and representation functions for the structured presentation of content. Within a single instructional module, "teaching" would take place through presentation of information and through student engagement in automated drill and practice exercises and tests related to that information (Rahmlow, 1980). Once education was reduced to structured content, testing protocols, and feedback mechanisms, the teacher became more or less superfluous as a professional subject. The computer was envisaged in functional analogy to the instructor and could be delegated work normally assigned to human beings.

CAI thus also allowed for an intensified division of labour across various points in the instructional process. CAI organised courses according to discrete blocs of information resources and system processes. The basic component of learning in systems like PLATO was the instructional unit, which consisted of a set of objectives, a body of information resources covering these objectives, test items designed around these resources, and a range of feedback mechanisms for guidance, performance evaluation and staging the learner's passage through the material. Such units were compiled together to create modules, which in turn were assembled into courses, which could be grouped to comprise curricula in different subjects areas. This modular structure both necessitated and was supported by a detail division of labour between course authors and instructors. Authors were charged with creating learning resources and performing those tasks which relate to subject matter expertise. These resources then became permanent and transferrable across all PLATO systems (Rahmlow et al., 1980). By contrast, "[t]he instructor's primary function [was] to select and administer curricula to students" (Rahmlow et al., 1980: 34). The modular organisation and management of course design and delivery thus drew upon the functional analysis of the teaching process to instantiate certain teacher functions in machines and to delegate professional practices across two distinct and hierarchically organised positions in a production and delivery model recognisable from other areas of technically rationalised activity.

So far we are well within the world of critics of educational media. However, if we limit our analysis to an interpretation of CAI as a commodified form of education, we obscure the processes through which computers came in the first place to be identified with the *potential for* and the *desirability of* such a form of education. To trace this history necessitates turning to a background of theoretical, pedagogical and organisational aspects of distance education.

A defining question for distance education in 1960s and 1970s was that of its relation to conventional teaching and learning. Addressing this question involved defining distance education either as a "mode" of education (subject to organisation, theorisation and evaluation with reference to conventional practices and forms), or as "a distinct field of educational endeavour," in which case theory, pedagogy, and organisation needed to be developed *ab ovo* (Keegan, 1996: 79). It is this second position that dominated the field during the early appropriation of the computer. The distinction in effect created a space of theorisation, practice and development to which conventional organisational and pedagogical modes were seen not to apply or to which they were seen as opposed. The source of the distinction is easily stated – the separation in space and time of the teacher and the student (Keegan, 1996; Moore, 1973; Peters, 1971). This basic condition ramifies into a fuller theorisation of distance education as a unique field. While a number of typologies emerged in the 1960s and 1970s, all share certain key features, which end up conditioning the way in which distance pedagogies develop and ultimately how media are appropriated into and developed for education:

- The learner is individualised – separate from the instructor, the institution and the learning group;
- Teaching is something to be delivered objectively – it must be placed in the sphere of the student, principally through materials and media;
- Instruction is subject to functional analysis – understood as a series of moments, each of which can be isolated and sequenced;
- The functions must be differentiated – once described, their performance can be redelegated across a range of system components;
- The institution must be the teacher – instruction must be co-ordinated and managed as a systemic activity subject to requirements of standardised production, economies of scale, technical efficiency and quality control.[11]

Beginning in the 1960s, but certainly by the mid-1970s, these points had become entrenched in distance education and aided in the construction of a distinct distance theory and pedagogy.

If the separation of the teacher and the student invited a remediation of instructional processes through objectified materials and machines, then a predicate for this was a thorough functional analysis of the instructional process and of the "teaching behaviours" that were now to be distributed. The pedagogical framework for this was supplied by an approach called "programmed instruction" developed in the 1960s and 1970s by Robert Gagne (Gagne, 1970). Programmed instruction is predicated on the behaviourist credo that learning is a process of behaviour modification affected through stimulus and response (Ally, 2004; Chen, 2006), and that the processes of learning can be planned logically into pre-established stages, allowing for reinforcement through regular exercises and tests (Orlich et al., 1990). At the heart of this approach is an analysis of teaching as a set of performances which can be isolated, described, broken down, and rationalised into simple functions. It should be emphasised that technology is not the basis of programmed instruction, but rather the latter provides goals, guidelines and a framework for imagining education as a mechanical activity, and so provides a foundation on which certain kinds of "teaching machines" can be designed and developed, on which the pedagogical potentials of technical tools and systems can be ascertained, and whereby the manner of their incorporation into education can be specified (c.f., Burton et al., 2004).

While programmed instruction supplied a foundation for the analysis of distributed instructional functions, three other aspects of the distance situation conditioned an appropriation of technology in a deskilled mode of education. These elements of the field can be summarised with reference to the work of Wedemeyer (1971), Moore (1973) and Holmberg (1986, 1983, 1978).

The separation of teacher and student means that learning takes place in conditions of much greater individual autonomy and independence than is the case in conventional settings. As such, these categories – autonomy and independence – become central to distance pedagogies, technologies and organisational strategies. Charles Wedemeyer sought to enhance autonomy and independence through distance teaching and learning processes. For Wedemeyer, the group learning typical of conventional education promotes conformity to the norms of the group as defined by the instructor rather than supporting real independence of thought. By contrast, distance education provides an environment in which greater control, autonomy and freedom over learning could and should be delegated to learners. The separation of teacher and student is seen here not only as a logistical problem, but as a basic precondition for an autonomous process focused around the independent self-activity of a student guided remotely via a technical medium (Wedemeyer, 1971). Autonomy and independence in the learner are qualities to be encouraged through the introduction of technologies supportive of *individualised* learning; and for their part, technical media gain value and are implemented in order to support individualisation and foster an educational practice predicated on the isolated individual as the basic unit in the educational relationship.

For Moore, the extension of learner autonomy and independence necessitates a parallel and pre-requisite extension to the learner of *control* over areas of education previously adjudicated by teachers, including such elements as the setting of learning objectives, choice of the methods of instruction, and even evaluation (Moore, 1973). The individualisation of teaching is thus also a matter of re-delegating agency across the teacher-student relationship so as to grant learners key *pedagogical* and *professional* functions of the instructor. Such an organisation of education corrects for the instructor's concentration of control over learning, while creating a need for distance institutions to "provide the appropriate structure of learning materials" to allow for a redelegation of control to learners (Moore & Kearsley, 1996: 205–6). In order to be integrated into this pedagogical framework, teaching materials and technical media must be designed and implemented to support (and presume) both learner autonomy and individualisation as well as the transfer of control over the education process from teachers to students.

The theory of independent, individualised learning and the basic conditions underlying it was effectively distilled in a pedagogical strategy developed by Holmberg and referred to as "guided didactic conversation" (Holmberg, 1986, 1983). Initiated by Holmberg's concern for limited interaction in distance learning, this strategy effectively supports individualisation and the redistribution of control by focusing on the possibility of *simulated interactivity* in teaching materials and media. Individualised learning necessitates an extension of control to the learner. But in order to achieve legitimacy as a forum for real learning, distance education must retain enough of a collective character to be distinguished from mere self-study. Distance education could maintain such a distinction, Holmberg claimed, by implementing a conversational relation between the student and the "tutorial organisation" (Holmberg, 1978). Holmberg surmised that this relationship did not have to take the form of a two-way interaction between student and instructor. It could instead be installed in materials and technical media which simulate interaction by making it a condition of learner engagements with such materials and media. Embedded in materials, interaction and conversation can be actualised by independent, individual students. The basic imperative of the design of materials for distance education is thus the incorporation of conversational and interactive elements that can simulate interactions between teacher and student. The correlate of this is that the concept of conversation must be translatable to the media utilised in distance education (Holmberg, 1986). As with programmed instruction, the notion of guided didactic conversation invites designers to look at educational materials and media as functional analogs for the teacher.

Predictably, the formalisation of these three elements – individualisation, control & simulated interaction – had an effect on the role of the teacher. Unlike in conventional education, where the act of teaching is summarised in a human figure whose performances disguise the institutional nexus that produces such performances, the acts of teaching in distance contexts are an explicit product of the relations between the various components comprising the system. At the extreme, teaching becomes a systemic performance. In the estimation of one early theorist, "[t]he world of distance education [...] has little of the characteristics of 'teaching' because there is, in general, no teacher in the system and the functions relating to student learning within the helping organisation are performed by a variety of machines, people, and materials" (Keegan, 1996: 58). Such an environment once again promotes a view technologies as functional elements within a cohesive and centrally co-ordinated process – a key aspect of the commodified form of CAI.

It should be noted that these pedagogical strategies and the technical media developed and deployed for actualising them took shape against particular features of the *organisation* of distance education. Once these features came to be subjected to rigorous analysis beginning in the 1960s, they were posited at the centre of a definition of distance education as an *industrial process* – a definition associated with the work of Otto Peters and that has had a powerful and lasting influence on theory, pedagogy, and institutional development in the field (Peters, 1994).

The separation of teacher and student correlates directly to a need to deliver individualised, self-paced, self-directed instruction to large numbers of students distributed over a wide area, a need to which the techniques of industrial mass production and distribution respond. However, this can only occur where learning materials themselves are produced and delivered as concrete objects, and where technical media are implemented to distribute such objects. These in turn require a mediating institution that can order the production, delivery and consumption of education via complex technical systems. Distance education is *rationalised* insofar as it is ordered around the mass production, distribution and consumption of commodified materials – "teaching," in Peters' words, "becomes an object which can be manipulated" (Peters, 1994: 205). The technical rationalisation of education enables forms of manipulation, duplication, analysis, measurement, accounting, and adaptation familiar from the production of industrial goods. The result is an intensive division and serial organisation of labour, as well as the necessity of a relatively autonomous, centralised co-ordinating body to evaluate and manage what is essentially an assembly line production process (Peters, 1994).

We have here the organisational foundations on the basis of which certain affordances of educational technologies come into focus and automated systems like CAI can be identified as logical and desirable. The functional analysis and breakdown of teaching enables the delegation of functions across its various moments in such a way as to stabilise a serial form of organisation in which technology has a clear role: in industrialised education "a technical device is used and takes over some of the functions of the teacher," or in a stronger formulation, a technical medium "teaches instead of the teacher" (Peters, 1994: 203). This should be understood not as an objective description, but a normative one – produced against a background that focuses attention on technology in a particular way and reveals certain of its potentials as desirable for actualisation.

The preceding analysis has attempted to show that the commodified form of computer-mediated education represented by CAI is not the result of the pure properties of computers. Rather, it was contingent on the convergence of pedagogical and institutional factors in the field of distance education which, taken together, comprised a "technical code" under the horizon of which understandings of the abstract value of the computer for education, assessments of its potential role and function in teaching and learning, and concrete applications such as CAI could take shape historically. The implication, of course, is that if "online education" is relative to a contingent background that shapes its formation, then alternative pedagogical, professional and institutional formations could produce alternative technical realisations. To test this, we turn to another case – that of early experiments in educational computer conferencing.

FROM COMMODIFICATION TO COMMUNICATION: COMPUTER CONFERENCING AT WBSI

In the early 1980s, when CAI was still the dominant mode of educational computing, a number of academically-based experiments tested educational applications of asynchronous, text-based computer conferencing. Successful online discussion groups of a more general, voluntary, and sometimes random sort had emerged prior to this on such services as The Source and CompuServe, but no attempt had yet been made at hosting a fully online education program. Educators critical of the deskilled information delivery model of CAI hoped to draw upon the capacity of conferencing systems to support group communication in order to realise a model of online education based on a dialogic pedagogy (Feenberg, 1993; Kaye, 1989; Kerr & Hiltz, 1982; Mason & Kaye, 1989). Among the early experiments were a series of teacher-training courses at the New Jersey Institute of Technology, some Adult Continuing Education courses at the New York Institute of Technology, the New School's ConnectEd program, and an experiment in mass education using computer conferencing at the Open University UK. The first organised online education program, however, was the School of Management and Strategic Studies (SMSS), which opened in January of 1982 at the Western Behavioural Sciences Institute (WBSI) in La Jolla, California.

The SMSS was a two-year executive education program dedicated to fostering critical humanistic dialogue around issues and problems of information societies in a rapidly globalizing economy. Participants came together at week-long biannual meetings at the Institute, but otherwise their only link with the program and one another was the Electronic Information Exchange System (EIES), the conferencing system employed in the SMSS. The program was divided into four semester-long courses, bracketed by the face-to-face meetings, with each course broken down into month-long seminars moderated by university faculty from all over the US. There were no assignments, no grades, and no certification – and yet despite the lack of the usual extrinsic motivations for study, the SMSS grew from a program with 8 initial participants, all but one in the US, to over 150 participants from over two dozen countries. So successful was the program that it was ranked in Harvard Business School's top 5 executive education programs (Meeks, 1987; Gottschalk, 1983).[12]

While the success of such a program might appear in hindsight only to confirm what everybody already knows about the "impacts" of new communication technologies in education – increased access and quality, user enthusiasm for flexible delivery methods, and the potentials of "virtualisation" – the SMSS owed less to the abstract properties of new technologies than to the way in which their affordances and limitations were interpreted through specific pedagogical and social values and actively appropriated. WBSI's faculty and staff realised from the start that computer conferencing was not a means of information delivery but a context for social interaction, communication and dialogue. However, since the medium was untried in education, no models for conducting an educational computer conference existed. Moreover, conferencing systems had not been designed with specifically educational applications in mind, but according to generic definitions of the communication process (Hiltz, 1994; WBSI, 1987). Faculty, staff and participants in the SMSS had to invent online education as they went along, negotiating between various notions of alternative pedagogy and the affordances and constraints of the conferencing medium.

Distributed, asynchronous, text-based communication is the primary mode of interaction afforded by computer conferencing. Today there is a standard discourse for describing the advantages of this mode of interaction: flexible anytime/ anywhere learning, increased time for formulating considered contributions, egalitarian communication in the absence of visible status markers, and so on. But in the practical contexts of the SMSS, these features of computer conferencing bore an ambivalent relationship to the education process. Distribution and asynchronicity also meant the absence of a ready-made and familiar context for learning and the devaluation of passive forms of participation that are perfectly legitimate in such contexts, where co-presence enables the easy flow of tacit communication. The verbal cues and situational norms that contextualise interaction in face-to-face settings are absent in a text-based medium, making it awkwardly opaque and even intimidating for new users (Feenberg, 1989). The ambivalence of these formal features of the technology raised a number of pedagogical challenges for faculty, staff and participants alike.

In CAI, learning is coded into the prescriptive structure of the system itself as a shell for organising content and evaluating student performances. Most contemporary learning management systems similarly provide a structure for the representation and delivery of content and the configuration of tools and applications. In computer conferencing, by contrast, there are no pre-determined prescriptions for learning at all – the system provides a structure for interaction and basic tools to facilitate communication, but no more. Conferencing systems do not replicate teaching functions, nor do they supply an explicit pattern for focused, cumulative or directed engagement with content – central elements of learning. There is no content, as far as the system is concerned, apart from the participants' contributions. However, regardless of the pure potential of the systems, interaction is by no means a given in the absence of technical prescriptions or social norms for participation.

Where a limited type of human-machine interaction is simply imposed by CAI, human to human interaction is a very real problem in computer conferencing – it is not pre-determined or prescribed technically, but has to be actively achieved. And, as was quickly discovered at WBSI, it had to be achieved in the absence of precedents. How do you achieve interaction, participation and focused dialogue in an environment where there are no explicit social norms, in which visual cues are absent, and in which none of the participants are together in the moment of interaction? Whereas CAI answered these questions by delegating teaching functions and roles to machines, at WBSI they were addressed through the innovation of communicative strategies. These strategies focused primarily on the development of techniques for moderating online discussion.

Arriving at these techniques was not an easy process. Two pedagogical approaches were tried in the early weeks of the SMSS. One approach was rooted in a belief that the open communication structure of the conferencing system required a "low-impact" moderator. It was presumed that student interest, independent of the conferencing context itself, would drive discussion as it had in other kinds of online forums, and that the provision of a space for communication would suffice to generate focused and meaningful interaction. Students, having completed a reading assignment, were asked to respond to the readings on the basis of very general questions. The questions were accompanied by a fleeting formal introduction to the course, the extent of which was "Greetings! Here we go." No context or background was supplied through which participants could understand how they might engage substantively in discussion. No norms were proposed through which the participants could understand their roles and responsibilities in this strange environment. And in the absence of the pressures of co-presence there was no particular compulsion to engage at all. Understandably, little participation resulted.

The other approach came from the opposite direction, assuming that the "emptiness" of the conferencing space needed to be filled with content to which the students could react. A series of lengthy introductory messages, analogous to a lecture, was sent out detailing the substantive focus of the seminar and followed up by a set of challenging problems to which participants were invited to respond. Whereas the "low-impact" approach did little to reduce the anxiety provoked by the blank computer screen, this "high-impact" approach increased the presence of the moderator to such a degree that it left little room for engagement. As a consequence, it inadvertently transformed the conferencing system into yet another vehicle for delivering content rather than facilitating discussion. Again, little active participation followed from this approach.

Unlike interest-based discussion forums, educational computer conferencing begged for the strong, active presence of a live teacher employing a self-conscious pedagogy. Participation was a function of the moderator's ability to both achieve and invite presence, to maintain coherence and direction, and to contextualise, both intellectually and socially, a highly ambiguous communication environment. The moderator had to take on contextualising, prompting, synthesising, and facilitating functions and an active leadership role in such a way as to provide enough structure to engage participation and enough openness to admit participants into dialogue (Feenberg, 1989; Kerr, 1984). Providing context and background, establishing the norms and expectations for interaction, outlining a program and a set of goals, and monitoring the progress of participants – standard dimensions of teaching in the off-line world – were thus reinterpreted in the conferencing medium as a means of facilitating and sustaining educational interaction.

But contrary to the division between "process" and "content" that informed CAI and the pedagogical and organisational frameworks underlying it, the moderator could not carry out these functions without being an expert in an academic field. Prompt responses to student questions and contributions were necessary in order to sustain the flow and coherence of dialogue in a context which tended towards fragmentation. But in the SMSS the dialogue itself consisted of humanistic inquiry into philosophical, social, and political-economic issues, as well as the historical and cultural backgrounds of emerging information societies. This called for an ability on the part of the moderator to evaluate and synthesise abstract concepts, provide historical background and context, and survey arguments within a field of inquiry.[13]

WBSI faculty soon realised, however, that here expertise bore a slightly different relation to the educational process than in the physical classroom. In order to maintain a coherent and directed flow of dialogue and a high level of participation, the synthetic, contextualising, and reflective activity of the moderator had to be more "punctual" than persistent, but no less incisive than in traditional educational contexts. Providing background and delineating the scope of a problem to be addressed, the moderator needed to guide discussion based on the contributions of the participants themselves. Expertise thus took on a quality of responsiveness in conferencing that it does not have in the information delivery models of computer-mediated education, where expertise is objectified in commodified content modules. With the computer in charge rather than a teacher, expert knowledge is programmed in before the education process actually begins and students simply respond to it as an unalterable context. Far from playing out an agenda of automation and commodification, however, WBSI's model of online education innovated an active social role for the instructor in response to the specific constraints and affordances of the conferencing medium.

So far our discussion seems to reinscribe the traditional antinomy of human and machine, focusing as it does on seemingly independent responses of users to the constraints of existing systems. But this cliché does not in fact describe the evolution of the WBSI experiment. It soon became obvious to the group that created the SMSS that they would also have to reinvent computer conferencing if their enterprise was to succeed – to engage directly, that is, in the process of technical innovation. The communicative functions of moderating needed to be accompanied by the development of technical features that could support both the functions themselves and WBSI's pedagogical model. This recognition arose from the problems encountered in using a generic communication technology for specifically educational purposes.

The generic interpretation of communication in conferencing systems failed to take account of how communication differs across social settings. Communication within educational contexts is clearly conducted with different purposes, expectations, roles, values, and norms than is dinner-table conversation within the family, debates at political meetings, or discussions among hobbyists about their hobbies, even if many of the same communication functions are at play. At the very least, CAI came with a model, however impoverished, of how education was to take place, assigning roles, establishing norms, and setting expectations in a coherent manner. Conferencing did not. The social and pedagogical functions of moderating at WBSI answered to and in part derived from this situation. But they also acted as a framework within which certain design features became desirable, and on the basis of which additional features could be innovated.

These features could be as simple as an ability to track individual participants' progress through the conference, allowing the moderator to better facilitate the conversation on the basis of a clear view of everybody's location within it (WBSI, 1987). They could be as complex as a subject indexing feature enabling both participants and moderators to follow different thematic threads and to weave these threads together at appropriate moments in summary comments useful for keeping the conversation on track (Feenberg, 1989). Experiments at WBSI with the latter feature failed for lack of sufficient computer power, but later inspired the Marginalia project discussed below. Social roles and practices did not develop out of the prior presence of these features. Rather the features were seen as desirable from within the purview of a particular social practice and pedagogical model.

Another major problem with early conferencing was the complexity of the user interface. It required a page of instructions just to sign on to EIES; and once online, the user was faced with lengthy sets of commands for operations as simple and taken-for-granted as writing, editing, quoting, sending and receiving, reading messages, printing, and attaching documents. The so-called "quick reference card" for EIES was 16 pages long (NJIT, 1986). The complexity of the system, however, was of a piece with its flexibility – in order to achieve as open and generic a communication environment as possible, designers merely added menus and command strings, to the point where flexibility seemed to reflect the needs and competencies of a narrow stratum of technical designers rather than students and teachers. The memorisation of non-intuitive command codes for the performance of intuitive social acts set a high bar for communication.

WBSI addressed this situation through the development of an original software application: a user-interface for educational computer conferencing called Passkey (WBSI, 1987, 1986). Similar to Web browsers, Passkey was designed as a simplified command interface layered over the more complex communication structure supplied by the conferencing system. Its effect, like the Web browser's for the Web, was to make the process of online communication more accessible to lay users, obviating the need to rely upon an abstruse set of commands for conducting communication online. Designed with the experience of both moderators and participants in the SMSS conferences in mind, Passkey represented a technical expression of the social, pedagogical and programmatic framework developed over the first four years of the program. Once again, the case exhibits not acquiescence to a given set of technical prescriptions, but the adaptation of technology to the needs of a specific user group.

The desire to enact a dialogic pedagogy, the development of social rather than technical delegations in response to technical constraints and practical challenges, and the undertaking of technological development in response and deference to local social values and expectations tells a much different story of online education than is often portrayed in mainstream debates. One reason for this difference lies in the proximity of both programmatic and technological development to the contexts of actual educational practice. Automation and commodification did not play as agendas in the SMSS, not only because the technology could not easily support them, but because the interests of instructors were directly present in the design and development contexts. The automation of certain moderating functions in educational computer conferences was suggested at NJIT, and implemented as another menu option, on the assumption that participation could most easily be achieved by building in technical features that would require it (Hiltz, 1982). If taken in that direction, the technology might have developed to support a similar agenda as information-delivery oriented CAI systems. But it was in providing an alternative to those systems that WBSI largely understood its work.

All in all, dynamic processes of negotiation and development between technical and social factors not only yielded an alternative model of online education, but in the present context, they also open up a range of questions for a critical politics of online education and university reform.

A REVISED POLITICS OF ONLINE EDUCATION

Educational technologies only gain definition, functionality and value in the framework of the pedagogical models they instantiate, the forms of social relationship they construct, and the institutional goals they are applied to achieve. The technologies only "work" within that model, those relationships, those goals, which supply a set of guidelines for what education in general is, and therefore for what form and role educational technologies should take. On an abstract, formal level, of course, it could be said that CAI and similar content-based educational systems "transform" education according to a pedagogical model that they themselves in a sense "possess." However, this model itself has its origins not in some abstract technological realm, but at the point where pedagogical, institutional, and social values and norms articulate with design principles, processes and parameters – the point, that is, at which such values and norms come to be translated into technically rational design features.[14] Indeed, the design of technologies is predicated on a prior definition of the situation to which technologies are to apply. Education must be defined in a social, functional and organisational sense before a technology can be developed – or even identified – to support it. The technology may embody a pedagogical model that carries certain political implications for society or career consequences for professional educators, but it only does so through an iterative process through which pedagogical assumptions, values and roles derived from the background of innovation, are delegated to technical systems.

Critical theory of technology calls this background of assumptions, values, definitions, and roles that guides technological development the "technical code" (Feenberg, 2002; 1991). Technical codes define a framework of decision-making within which certain design choices appear rational and desirable. These codes are a function of the delineation and circumspection of technological development and design by particular social groups to whose interests the ultimate form of technology is relative. Such groups may not bear an explicit "ideology" or identifiable reform strategy, but they will, by and large, bias the design process relative to the subjective horizons within which they define the world of social practice to which their work is addressed. The technical code of online education, then, is relative to the interests, assumptions and values of the actors who are engaged in the design and development process, and who are thus positioned as powerful interpreters of the both technology and the social practice it mediates.

CAI, as the above case indicates, is not simply a logical derivation from the abstract properties of computers. It is the product of an interpretation of the educational potentials of the computer which takes shape against a specific historical, social, intellectual, and institutional background – one derived from a particular field and the perennial concerns, conflicts, and issues that define that field. If CAI actualises certain potentials of the computer this is not because of The Computer itself, but because the field within which these potentials are identified already privileges a concern with the representation and delivery of information and with pedagogies centred on the production of commodified materials, the conduct of automated process, and division of labour. CAI is actualised at the intersection of technical potentials and a framework for interpreting those potentials that pushes development towards automated and commodified forms. Computer conferencing, as the WBSI case illustrates, opened a completely different interpretive field for computer-mediated education in highlighting the functionality of the computer as a communications device. The alternative pedagogy developed at WBSI was not so much the result of the formal properties of computer conferencing as it was an appropriation of those properties within a subjectively defined set of priorities, choices, and goals. Conferencing's formal ambivalence with respect to education was addressed at WBSI through both social and technical adaptations aimed at achieving an active, dialogic online pedagogy. Automation was never an option, not because technical limitations at that early date precluded it, but because it was never a value for the developers of the SMSS program. It was incompatible with the technical code out of which WBSI's model of online education emerged.

Computer conferencing and CAI, then, are not just two different uses of the same technology, but supply two completely different paths for the educational appropriation of the computer. They draw upon and support two completely different pedagogical models. They delegate interaction in education in completely different ways. And they operate on two completely different dimensions of the social process of education. Automation and commodification, far from being inevitable consequences of online education, must be understood as contingent outcomes whose realisation is dependent on a particular configuration of the technology and a particular set of pedagogical choices. Here, as elsewhere, the crucial philosophical and political questions to be asked are: what does the technology stand in for in the education process; how is it involved in delegating functions across that process; and how is a field of social interests delineated to encourage one iteration over other possibilities?

In information-centric iterations of computer-mediated education like CAI, the technology is designed to stand in for the teacher, to enable a technical performance of the functions of human professionals. It is this that aligns it with a program of automation. Communication-centred models of online education present a very different scenario. Here the technology stands in for the classroom as an environment for interaction, dialogue, and the formation of community. Rather than taking on a functional role within the education process, it provides a more or less flexible structure for the negotiation of familiar social roles. Functional delegations are not simply built into the technology, but are actively configured out of a combination of social and technical options that, as in the case of the SMSS, include a role for the professional teacher.

Technologies, educational or otherwise, do not autonomously transform the social contexts to which they are introduced, though their influence in giving shape and substance to those contexts is considerable. Certainly writing transformed the process of learning, but it did not replace dynamic interaction with static information-gathering, as Plato predicted. Over the centuries, educators and students have managed to devise ways of situating writing within interactive social processes. Writing has added its capacities as an information technology to the communicative processes of teaching and learning in ways that are now so obvious and taken-for-granted that they are barely noted. Networked computing also provides a powerful means of organising, representing and transmitting information, but to limit it to these capacities is to ignore its potential as a communications medium. The integration of technology into education is, however, ongoing, and its ultimate form is not yet decided. There is still time for intervention and redirection in accordance with academic values and interests. Whether a positive evolution of the technology will emerge will depend, in part, upon the ability of academics themselves to move beyond the static oppositions and absolute positions that have characterised debates around online education.

QUESTIONS OF EDUCATIONAL TECHNOLOGY

What are the implications of this analysis for technological design? In the early 1980s, the "interpretative flexibility" (Pinch & Bijker, 1984) of computer networking was very great. CAI might have been a dominant mode of educational computing, but it was relatively easy for new actors with different goals to take up the project of online education and direct it to different ends. By the early 1990s, the pedagogical and technical model developed in the early conferencing experiments seemed poised to become what online education would be. However, with the coincidence of the wider diffusion of the Web and mounting fiscal and legitimacy crises in higher education, a boost was given to the earlier discourse of automation, which could now repackage itself in terms of the kinds of dynamic online pedagogy that those at WBSI had innovated. This was not primarily *social interaction*, but (as with CAI) a kind of *automated "interactivity"* that enabled what appeared as an easy *rapprochement* between strategies of automation and the questions of pedagogical quality that have consistently undermined efforts at deskilling in education. Very rapidly, this new conception of the field was reflected in the design of enterprise Learning Management Systems (LMS), such as WebCT and Blackboard, that have now become fixtures on North American campuses. Online education became "successful," and in many of the same terms as the early experiments; but now it was tied to a project of deskilling that was fundamentally antithetical to the ethos of those experiments.

LMS generally emphasise the representational rather than the relational affordances of networked computers. Often, but not always, a Web forum, equivalent to the computer conferences of old, is included in the product but given less attention by trainers preparing instructors to use the new technology. The interpretation of online education resisted by Noble and others was effectively inscribed in its technical code to the extent that this was technically feasible and politically desirable. In response, resistance to online education has tended to accept this code as inevitable, mistaking a particular social design for the essence of the technology itself.

The WBSI case takes on its full significance against this background. True, educational conferencing never achieved the widespread usage of the current systems. But it represents an existence proof of the alternative. It demonstrates the concrete possibility of another line of development that would emphasise relational potentials rooted in traditional pedagogical conceptions shared by most faculty rather than the budgetary concerns of administrators and commercial strategists. The single most important constraint that flows from this alternative is small classes, manageable by a living professor, rather than huge audiences or markets for semi-automated educational "products." In this form, online education must defend its value on a pedagogical basis because it cannot significantly contribute to cheapening education or creating new revenue streams around educational commodities. There is no "business model" for learning as traditionally conceived, even when the classroom is virtual.

This line of development, too, is inscribed in a technical code. Insofar as the movement for open source educational software depends on faculty input and support, this technical code is likely to emerge as its agenda. To illustrate this point, we will briefly describe three initiatives in this field.

One complaint about online education is that it has largely been taken over by commercial software developers. This tends to mean that universities are signing off on expensive licensing agreements and putting themselves at the whim of the companies who offer web-based educational services. Universities buy into a "one-size-fits-all" model of online education that is largely shaped in the image of a corporate conception of what education is and means. In many ways, the commercial mode of technological development in online education fosters the automated, commodified model attacked by the critics of educational technology, and can thus be identified as an evolution in the model of online education initiated in CAI.

Open source software development can go a long way to resolving these issues by opening development processes to a wider group of potential innovators than is available to even a very large commercial enterprise, allowing universities to internalise innovation to the communities that the technical systems themselves are meant to serve (Green, 2004). Of course, some might question the viability of such an approach – in the first place, who in their right mind would engage in the development of software solely on a voluntary basis with no guarantee of compensation. For another thing, is it not the case that the kind of unorganised, decentralised innovation process on which open source depends will result in substandard products or immense duplication? The answer to both questions is rooted in the ideals of community on the basis of which both open source development and (to some degree) academic culture are based. The example of Moodle, an open source, community-developed learning management system, can help to illustrate this.

Moodle[15] is an open source LMS developed in Australia by Martin Dougiamas and first rolled out beyond experimental contexts in 2003 (Dougiamas & Taylor, 2003). The system has a similar modular design as other LMS, but its open license means that geographically distributed end-users can introduce new functionality as well as modify the existing tool set without hampering other users' implementations of the software. This *technical* difference is a product of a key *philosophical* difference in the way that Dougiamas imagined Moodle to relate to educational processes (Dougiamas, 1998). From its inception, Moodle was not designed simply to manage course content or those functions which relate to administrative and informational functions of teaching and learning. Moodle does, indeed, offer these facilities, but the logic of its organisation stresses the interrelation between teachers and students as a communicative and collaborative one. As the technology has developed through the hands of its large communicaty development network, a range of features supporting social interaction – forums, blogs, collaborative authoring tools and so on – have been introduced and also proven to be the more commonly used applications on the system. Indeed, it is a combination of the diffusion of the development initiative among the Moodle community and the nature of that community which could be said to have produced this developmental trajectory. This is because, by and large, the openness of Moodle allows for a closer collaboration between the practices and philosophies of professional teachers in the classroom and the technical resources available on campus in the creation of usable applications. Developers have incentive to create applications not because they are earning a wage, but because it is an extension of their normal work as salaried members of academic institutions. As a result, the applications that are developed are more likely to reflect the logic not of efficiency and expediency, but the values of practitioners with an interest in developing pedagogical practice. The success of this venture is reflected in Moodle's rapid growth over the last 8 years – as of this writing (2011), Moodle has over 54,000 registered sites in 212 countries, hosts about 4.5-million courses, and claims over 43-million users.[16]

An example of the flexibility of the open source development model is a recently developed annotation tool called Marginalia.[17] Developed by Andrew Feenberg, Geoff Glass and Cindy Xin at Simon Fraser University in Vancouver, Marginalia integrates with Web-based discussion forums (specifically, for Moodle) and addresses key pedagogical problems with online discussion: specifically, their tendency to fragment into monologue and to be seen as peripheral to the real substance of courses. Its aim is to allow instructors and students to add side-bar commentary to ongoing online discussion and to annotate other forms of web-text. It supports one of the key moderating functions identified in the WBSI experiment of the early 1980s – that is, synthesising the contributions to online discussion in relation to overarching course themes, concepts, materials, or learning objectives. As such, it is a direct extension of the discursive model of online education developed at WBSI and an example of the direction in which online education can go if the capacity for innovation is distributed to those most deeply involved and invested in the education process.

On a much larger scale, the Sakai project[18] is a community source software development project founded by the University of Michigan, Indiana University, MIT, Stanford, the uPortal Consortium and the Open Knowledge Initiative with the support of the Andrew K. Mellon Foundation. Sakai has, among other things, developed an open source LMS, the first version of which was released in July, 2004. In addition to providing open source online education tools and applications, Sakai has also developed a Tool Portability Protocol which provides universities with a framework to develop and share software under the Sakai license. While the Sakai license does not prohibit the commercialisation of its software, it ensures that the knowledge base on which such developments are made remains open and sharable. Universities are thus able to retain a much greater level of control over development, adoption, support and implementation than is possible with commercial systems. Like Moodle, this project promises to free online education, at least in past, from the commercial control of systems development and thus commercial direction of the form of online education.

The current state of online education is deeply ambiguous. Administrations have had to temper their ambitions as they discovered that technology is not capable of delivering on the promise of cost-effectiveness without severely degrading educational quality. This was a prospect resisted by both faculty and students, notably in the California State University system where demonstrations at the State legislature and resolutions by faculty senates blocked a corporate sponsored attempt to "wire" the campuses. But before this realisation had sunk in, universities invested millions in the infrastructure of online education. The basic software acquired and developed in this context and used now on most campuses retains the representational emphasis and reflects the automating agenda of the commercial vendors who originally drove this process with unrealistic promises.

Meanwhile, faculty often, if not always, appropriate the available systems for a familiar pedagogical practice that combines representation of content (the online equivalent of textbooks or lectures) with the active use of a Web forum and other collaborative tools (the online equivalent of classroom discussion). This is precisely the sort of thing envisaged at WBSI thirty years ago. But these practices are not often supported by corresponding reductions in teaching loads and class sizes to render the interactive online pedagogy truly comparable with classroom teaching in terms of burden and effort. This confusing state of affairs may slowly give way to a satisfactory synthesis if open source initiatives are successful and faculty organisations vigilant. This is the outcome towards which we should work rather than resisting online education as such.

CONCLUSION: POLICY AND DESIGN

The essential question to ask in a revised politics of online education is whether the technology will work to facilitate the transmission of static information, fostering standardised modes of interaction between users, machines and commodified knowledge, or whether the technologies and online programs can be rooted in an essentially dialogic form of education, extending and enabling interaction within a similar professional structure. Technology could potentially support either one of these programs. But, as outcomes, they are in no sense given prior to specific appropriations within particular social settings.

Struggles over technological change take place in contexts that have their own political, social and historical dynamics, and that provide their own affordances for action, authority and intervention. The university is no exception. It is a complex institution organised around an administrative core whose relative power has increased significantly over the past half-century, but in which there is still a strong tradition of professional self-governance and participatory decision-making. Despite the growing discretionary power of both administrative bodies and state/corporate entities, faculty and students still have some power in the institution and can intervene in institutional change. Policy developments with respect to educational technologies and distance education show that the critique of online education can and must include an account of interventions through the community-based structures of the university and professional associations. These latter have accounted for the incorporation of faculty interests into online education. They are also important sites for the enactment and analysis of an alternative critical politics of online education.

The American Association of University Professors (AAUP) and the Canadian Association of University Teachers (CAUT) have issued position statements on online and distance education that act as an important basis for local faculty interventions in the appropriation of educational technologies.[19] In the case of CAUT, these statements address issues of commercialisation, privatisation and deprofessionalisation. By framing their position with respect to particular social issues, CAUT establishes a basis for the alternative development of online education and promotes critical engagement by local institutions in the appropriation of educational technologies.

The AUPP statement on distance education is framed in terms of the disjuncture between academic policies governing more traditional modes of distance education and network technologies. Recognition that the latter have the capacity to do something fundamentally different from the old correspondence school model and CAI suggests that they ought to be designed to better conform to academic values and priorities. Academic freedom, free access to information, freedom of teaching, intellectual property rights, and so on are central to the position statement and outline clearly the need to embed new technologies and online programs in traditional professional interests and institutional structures. The responsibility for developing online education is situated within the academic community as a whole, with recognition that new technologies must be integrated into education through the normal academic channels.

But do these position statements have any impact on local institutional policy? We have not surveyed the broad spectrum of institutions adopting new technologies, but here at least is a significant example of the sort of developments we hope are widespread. San Diego State University's faculty senate has developed a comprehensive distance education policy that addresses the issues of automation, commercialisation and deskilling.[20] The policy grounds the development of distance education in the traditional mission, governance, decision-making structures, and value frameworks of the university. The policy mandates that distance education technologies be evaluated according to traditional pedagogical and professional principles, and that the relationship with external organisations providing courseware and technology be open to scrutiny by faculty committees. Most important, the policy requires that both educational technologies and distance programs be organised in a way that respects faculty autonomy, academic freedom, and intellectual property. The policy also contains guidelines for employment of adjunct and part-time non-tenured faculty, and thus engages directly and proactively with one of the main points of political contention in debates over online education – its role in the deprofessionalisation of university teaching.

These policies and position statements provide a framework for the development and implementation of online education and educational technologies *within* the values, norms and expectations that typify universities as professional organisations. They strengthen the alternative technical code of online education worked out in early computer conferencing by placing that code within the larger organisational and institutional frameworks of universities and professional associations. And they address the concerns of online education's most vehement critics, internalising critical discourse to the decision-making process around educational technology.

In the wake of the general disappointment with the exaggerated claims made for online education, there is now wide latitude for faculty intervention and participation in shaping the terms on which it will impact the academic labour process, the division of academic labour, and ownership of intellectual resources. It is now clear that online education will not destroy the university as we know it. What it will become will be determined ultimately by the politics of the very institution it promised to replace only a few short years ago.

NOTES

[1] Contrast this evangelism with the contemporary language of "blended learning" or "instructional enhancement."

[2] It is ironic that when, in the mid-1980s, the Western Behavioural Sciences Institute invited Peter Drucker to speak to the first online education program, he had his secretary send back a pre-printed card declining the invitation. Apparently it took a while for this futurologist to see the future and even then his vision turned out to be slightly blurred.

[3] C.f., Bates (2004, 2000), Duderstadt (1999), Inglis (2002), Katz & Oblinger (2000), Naidu (2003), Smith (2002), Steeples & Jones (2002).

[4] C.f., Aronowitz (1999), Levidow (2002), Moll (2001, 1997), Robbins & Webster (1999), Schiller (1999).

[5] C.f., Callon & Latour (1981), Feenberg (2002), Latour (1995, 1994, 1991), Pinch & Bijker (1984), Winner (1986).

[6] C.f. Cornford & Pollack (2003), Gunawardena & McIsaac (2004), Feenberg (2002, 1999a, 1993), Robbins & Webster (2002).

[7] Feenberg (2002, 1999b, 1995, 1991)

[8] C.f., Blake & Standish (2000), Robins & Webster (2002).

[9] C.f. Alessi & Trollip (1985), Buchanan (2004), Cotton (1991), Darack (1977), Pagliaro (1983), Rahmlow et al., (1980), Woolley (1994).

[10] The acronym is often thought to stand for "Programmed Logic for Automated Teaching Operations," though neither its original designers nor the Control Data Corporation ever formally acknowledged this attribution. C.f., McNeil (n.d.) and Rahmlow et al., (1980).

[11] Gunawardena & McIsaac, 2004; Kaye, 1988; Keegan, 1996; Peters, 1994.

[12] For a more detailed account of the structure and legacy of the SMSS, see Feenberg (1999b, 1993).

[13] For an account of the relation of communicative and intellectual functions in educational conferencing, see Xin (2003).

[14] C.f. Feenberg (2002, 1999b, 1995, 1991).

[15] C.f., www.moodle.org.

16 C.f., http://moodle.org/stats/ for current figures.
17 C.f., http://webmarginalia.net/
18 C.f., www.sakaiproject.org.
19 C.f., www.aaup.org & http://www.caut.ca.
20 C.f., http://www.sfu.ca/~andrewf/sdsudisted.html

REFERENCES

Alessi, S.M. & Trollip, S.R. (1985). *Computer-based instruction: Methods and development.* Englewood Cliffs, NJ: Prentice-Hall.

Ally, M. (2004). Foundations of educational theory for online learning. In T. Anderson & F. Elloumi (Eds.). *Theory and practice of online learning.* Athabasca, AB: Athabasca University. 3–31.

Aronowitz, S. (1999). *The knowledge factory: Dismantling the corporate university and creating true higher education.* Boston: Beacon.

Bates, A.W. (2000). *Managing technological change: Strategies for college and university leaders.* San Francisco: Jossey-Bass.

Blake, N. & Standish, P. (2000). *Inquiries at the interface: Philosophical problems of online education.* Oxford: Oxford UP.

Burton, J.K., Moore, D.M. & Magliaro, S. (2004). Behaviorism and instructional technology. In D.H. Jonassen (Ed.). *Handbook of research on educational communications and technology* 2nd ed. Mahwah, NJ: Lawrence Erlbaum. 3–35.

Callon, M. & Latour, B. (1981). Unscrewing the big Leviathan: How actors macro structure reality and how sociologists help them to do so. In K. Knorr-Cetina & A.V. Cicourel (Eds.). *Advances in social theory and methodology: Toward an integration of micro- and macro-sociologies.* London: Routledge and Keegan Paul. 277–303.

Chen, I. (2006). *An electronic textbook on instructional technology.* Accessed: July 24, 2007 from http://viking.coe.uh.edu/~ichen/ebook/et-it/cover.htm.

Cornford, J. & Pollock, N. (2003). Putting the university online: Information, technology and organisational change. Philadelphia, PA: Society for Research into Higher Education and Open UP.

Darack, A. (1977). Yes...Computers can revolutionize education, *Consumer digest,* Sept.-Oct., 1977. Accessed: July 17, 2007 from www.xmn.com/images/plato%20chapter%20cons%20rept.pdf.

Dougiamas, M. (1998). A journey into constructivism. Accessed: June 26, 2008 from http://dougiamas.com/writing/constructivism.html#background.

Dougiamas, M. & Taylor, P.C. (2003). Moodle: Using learning communities to create an open source course management system. Accessed: June 26, 2008 from http://dougiamas.com/writing/edmedia2003/.

Duderstadt, J. (1999). Can colleges and universities survive in the information age? In R. Katz & Associates (Eds.). *Dancing with the devil: Information technology and the new competition in higher education.* San Francisco: Jossey-Bass. 1–25.

Feenberg, A. (2002). *Transforming technology: A critical theory revisited.* Oxford: Oxford UP.

Feenberg, A. (1999a). Wither educational technology? *Peer Review* 1(4). Online: http://www.sfu.ca/~andrewf/peer4.html.

Feenberg, A. (1999b). *Questioning technology.* London: Routledge.

Feenberg, A. (1995). *Alternative modernity: The technical turn in philosophy and social theory.* Berkeley: University of California Press.

Feenberg, A. (1993). Building a global network: The WBSI experience. In L. Harasim (Ed.). *Global networks: Computers and international communication.* Cambridge, MA: The MIT Press. 185–197.

Feenberg, A. (1991). *Critical theory of technology.* Oxford: Oxford UP.

Feenberg, A. (1989). The written world: On the theory and practice of computer conferencing. In R. Mason & T. Kaye (Eds.). *Mindweave: Communication, computers, and distance education.* Oxford: Pergamon Press. 22–39.

Gagné, R.M. (1970). *The conditions of learning.* 2nd ed. New York: Holt, Rinehart & Winston.

Gottschalk, E.C. (1983). California Institute uses 'teleconferences' to teach business strategy, computer use. *The Wall St. Journal.* Feb. 10, 1983. 33.

Green, K.C. (2004). Sakai and the four C's of open source. *Campus Technology,* Feb. 27, 2004. Syllabus Media Group. Accessed: March 29, 2005 from http://campustechnology.com/chapters/39707/.

Gunawardena, C.N. & McIsaac, M.S. (2004). Distance education. In D. Jonassen (Ed.). *Handbook of research on educational communication and technology.* Mahwah, NJ: Lawrence Erlbaum. 355–395.

Hiltz, S.R. (1994). *The virtual classroom: Learning without limits via computer networks.* Norwood, NJ: Ablex.

Hiltz, S.R. (1982). Comment CC14: 21 Feb., 1982. IN E. Kerr *Computers in education.* Unpublished computer conference transcript. NJIT: EIES, C303.

Holmberg, B. (1986). A discipline of distance education. *Journal of Distance Education.* Accessed, Aug. 7, 2007: http://cade.athabascau.ca/vol1.1/holmberg.html.

Holmberg, B. (1983). Guided didactic conversation in distance education In D. Stewart, D. Keegan & B. Holmberg (Eds.). *Distance education: International perspectives.* London: Croom Helm. 114–122.

Holmberg, B. (1978). Practice in distance education – a conceptual framework. *Canadian Journal of University Continuing Education* 6(1). 18–30.

Inglis, A., Ling, P. & Joosten, V. (2002). *Delivering digitally: Managing the transition to knowledge media.* 2nd ed. Open and Distance Learning Series. London: Kogan Page.

Katz, R. & Oblinger, D. (2000). *The 'e' is for everything: E-commerce, e-business and e-learning in the future of higher education.* Educause Leadership Strategies 2. San Francisco: Jossey-Bass; Educause; Pricewaterhourse Coopers.

Kaye, T. (1989). Computer-mediated communication and distance education. In R. Mason & T. Kaye (Eds.). *Mindweave: Communication, computers and distance education.* Oxford: Pergamon. 3–21.

Kaye, A. (1988). Distance education: The state of the art. *Prospects* 18:1. 43–54.

Keegan, D. (1996). *Foundations of distance education,* 3rd ed. Routledge Studies in distance Education. London: Routledge Falmer.

Kerr, E.B. (1984). Moderating online conferences. Computerised Conferencing & Communications Center, Research Report #20. Newark, NJ: New Jersey Institute of Technology.

Kerr, E.B. & Hiltz, S.R. (1982). *Computer-mediated communication systems: Status and evaluation.* New York: Academic Press.

Kinzer, C.K., Sherwood, R.D. & Bransford, J.D. (1986). *Computer strategies for education.* Columbus, OH: Merrill Publishing Co.

Kittler, F. (2004). Universities: Wet, hard, soft & harder. *Critical Inquiry* 31(1). 244–256.

Latour, B. (1995). Mixing humans and non-humans together: The sociology of a door closer. In S.L. Star (Ed.). *Ecologies of knowledge: Work and practices in science and technology.* Albany: SUNY Press. 257–277.

Latour, B. (1994). On technical mediation: Philosophy, sociology, genealogy. *Common knowledge.* 3. 29–64.

Latour, B. (1991). Technology is society made durable. In J. Law (Ed.). *A sociology of monsters: Essays on power, technology, and domination.* London: Routledge. 103–131.

Lenzner & Johnson (1997). Seeing things as they really are. Interview with Peter Drucker. *Forbes Magazine* (March 10, 1997). http://www.forbes.com/forbes/1997/0310/5905122a.html.

Levidow, L. (2002). Marketizing higher education: Neoliberal strategies and counter-strategies. *The commoner,* no. 3 (January, 2002). http://www.commoner.org.uk/previous_issues.htm#n3.

Lyotard, J.-F. (1984). *The postmodern condition: A report on knowledge.* G. Bennington & B. Masumi (Trans.). Theory and History of Literature 10. Minneapolis: University of Minnessota Press.

Mason, R. & Kaye, T. (Eds.). (1989). *Mindweave: Communications, computers and distance education.* Oxford: Pergamon Press.

McNeil, S. (n.d.) *A hypertext history of instructional design.* Accessed, July 3, 2007: http://www.coe.uh.edu/courses/cuin6373/idhistory/index.html.

Meeks, B. (1987). The quiet revolution: Online education becomes a real alternative. *Byte.* February, 1987. (183–190).

Moll, M. (Ed.). (2001). *But it's only a tool! The politics of technology and education reform.* Proceedings, American Educational Research Association (AERA). Montreal, 1999. Ottawa: Canadian Centre for Policy Alternatives.

Moll, M. (Ed.). (1997). *Tech high: Globalization and the future of Canadian education.* Ottawa: Canadian Centre for Policy Alternative & Fernwood Publishing.

Moore, M. (1973). Toward a theory of independent learning and teaching. *Journal of Higher Education.* 44. 661–679.

Moore, M.G. & Kearsley, G. (1996). *Distance education: A systems view.* Belmont, CA: Wadsworth.

Naidu, S. (Ed.). (2003). *Learning and teaching with technology: Principles and practices.* London: Kogan Page.

New Jersey Institute of Technology. (1986). Electronic Information Exchange System: Quick reference card. Jersey City, NJ: NJIT.

Noble, D. (2002). *Digital diploma mills: The automation of higher education.* Toronto: Between the Lines Press.

Orlich, D.C., Harder, R.J., Callahan, R.C. & Gibson, H.W. (1985). *Teaching strategies: A guide to better instruction.* Lexington, MA: D.C. Heath.

Pagliaro, L.A. (1983). The history and development of CAI: 1926–1981, an overview. *The Alberta journal of educational research.* 29(1). 75–84.

Peters, O. (1994). *Otto Peters on distance education: The industrialization of teaching and learning.* D. Keegan (Ed.). London: Routledge.

Peters, O. (1971). Theoretical aspects of correspondence instruction. In O. MacKenzie & E. Christiansen (Eds.). *The changing world of correspondence study.* University Park: Pennsylvania State University Press. 223–228.

Pinch, T. & Bijker, W. (1984). The social construction of facts and artifacts: Or how the sociology of science and the sociology of technology might benefit each other. *Social Studies of Science* 14(3). 399–441.

Plato. (1973). *Phaedrus and Letters VII and VIII.* London: Penguin.

Rahmlow, H.F., Fratini, R.C. & Ghesquiere, J.R. (1980). *PLATO.* Instructional Design Library vol. 30. Englewood Cliffs, NJ: Educational Technology Publications.

Robbins, K. & Webster, F. (Eds.). (2002). *The virtual university? Knowledge, markets, and management.* Oxford: Oxford UP.

Robbins, K. & Webster, F. (1999). *Times of the technoculture: From the information society to the virtual life.* London Routledge.

Schiller, D. (1999). *Digital capitalism: Networking the global market system.* Cambridge, MA: The MIT Press.

Smith, N. (2002). Teaching as coaching: Helping students to learn in a technological world. *Educause Review* May/June, 2002. 38–47.

Smith, S.E. (1957). Educational structure: The English-speaking Canadian universities. In C. Bissell (Ed.). *Canada's crisis in higher education.* Toronto: University of Toronto Press. 8–22.

Steeples, C. & Jones, C. (Eds.). (2002). *Networked learning: Perspectives and issues.* Computer Supported Co-operative Work Series. London: Springer.

Wallhaus, R.A. (2000). E-learning: From institutions to providers, from students to learners. In R. Katz & D. Oblinger. *The 'e' is for everything: E-commerce e-business and e-learning in the future of higher education.* Educause Leadership Strategies 2. San Francisco: Jossey-Bass; Educause; Pricewaterhouse Coopers. 21–52.

Wedemeyer, C. (1971). Independent study. In L. Deighton (Ed.). *The Encyclopaedia of Education.* Vol. 4. New York: Macmillan. 548–557.

Werry, C. (2001). The work of education in the age of e-college. *First Monday,* Vol. 6 No. 5 (May, 2001). Accessed March, 22, 2004 from http://www.firstmonday.dk/issues/issue6_5/werry/.

Western Behavioral Sciences Institute. (1987). *Social factors in computer mediated communication.* Report prepared for Digital Equipment Corporation. May 30, 1987.

Western Behavioral Sciences Institute. (1986). *Proposal for the creation of a computer-mediated social systems research and development program at the Western Behavioral Sciences Institute jointly with the Digital Equipment Corporation.* Proposal submitted to the Digital Equipment Corporation, May, 1986.

Winner, L. (1986). *The whale and the reactor. A search for limits in an age of high technology.* Chicago: University of Chicago Press.

Woolley, D.R. (1994). PLATO: The emergence of online community. *Computer mediated communication magazine.* 1(3). Accessed, July 17, 2007: http://www.ibiblio.org/cmc/mag/1994/jul/plato.html.

Wulf, W. A. (1998). University alert: The information railroad is coming. *Virginia.edu* 2:2 (Fall, 1998). http://www.itc.virginia.edu/virginia.edu/fall98/mills/comments/c1.html.

III. THE CIVIC INTERNET

NORM FRIESEN, ANDREW FEENBERG, GRACE SMITH,
AND SHANNON LOWE

EXPERIENCING SURVEILLANCE

A Phenomenological Approach

INTRODUCTION: PHENOMENOLOGY AND SURVEILLANCE STUDIES[1]

In response to the increasingly quotidian, even banal character of surveillant practices in postindustrial societies, this chapter explores the possibility of a theoretical and methodological re-alignment in surveillance studies. This re-alignment entails a move from broadly Foucauldian, macro-level, structural or poststructural analyses, to the existential–phenomenological study of subjective consciousness and experience. This piece illustrates such an experiential study by taking part of Sartre's famous description of "the look," and comparing it to a similarly experientially based description of an everyday context of surveillance—specifically, a bank machine or ATM transaction. Through the analysis of these descriptions, the piece shows how the study of the lived experience of surveillance highlights the role of the body, of social convention, and also of individual agency in surveillant practices that can be overlooked in other analyses.

In everyday experience, we engage in transactions, fill out forms, create online profiles, pass through security checks, and participate in myriad other situations in which our movements are registered, our identities verified, and the minutiae of our lives recorded. The vicissitudes of these everyday experiences reveal an ambivalent mix of freedom and control or security and uncertainty.

Facebook for example, the dominant, online social media communication platform at the time of writing, proffers extensive possibilities for new forms of communicating within strict constraints. The primarily commercial site is perhaps a consummate example of how a combination of commercial interests, government use and control, and unpredicted affordances for inter-personal/international communication manufacture a distinctive ambivalence in the use of new communication technology. While one must relinquish privacy (in the form of profile information that Facebook owns and that may be turned over to the authorities), and submit to relentless 'direct to socialiser' advertising with pin-point precision, in order to have the freedom to communicate, in return, users may put their account to any number of uses. Facebook seems to have played a critical role in protests against governments in Tunisia, Egypt and elsewhere, for example. The site's role in the so-called Arab Spring of 2011 could justify an extensive study. When we turn to the footage and stills of Tahrir square in February, 2011 or earlier developments in Tunisia (December, 2010), we see the platform being hailed by some activists

A. Feenberg and N. Friesen (eds.), (Re)Inventing the Internet: Critical Case Studies, 73–84.

leaders as an emancipatory technology. Signs thanking Mark Zuckerberg, Facebook's founder, for example, appeared in both Egypt and Tunisia. On the other hand, government counter-measures against social web activism in these same places are well known: Egyptian ex-President Hosni Mubarak shut off the Internet and the Tunisian government reportedly blocked some Internet addresses and users and created others for the purposes of manipulation and entrapment.

This recent activity on or through a prominent communication site indicates the technology's deeply ambivalent mix of freedom and constraint. On the one hand, the Internet and other forms of data transmission— coupled with cameras, databases, detectors, etc.—do not simply track us, they also change the way we see ourselves, the way we are in the world. This is sometimes called the "subject-forming" or "subjectivating" effect of surveillance. It has received theoretical treatment in a wide range of texts referencing Michel Foucault's early analyses of panoptic and other controlling structures. On the other hand, these subject-forming social mechanisms do not generally produce the pathological consequences evoked in such analyses of surveillance. We are not, as a rule, reduced to disciplined performance or rendered clinically paranoid by the panoptic power of omnipresent security cameras, motion detectors, and myriad other tracking and recording devices. But how can an account of the ambivalences of surveillance in our everyday life be articulated? Such an articulation would involve consideration not only of the subject-forming powers of the mechanisms of surveillance and dataveillance, but also of the *interiority* of the corresponding forms of subjectivity.

When Foucault was looking into the role of surveillance and control in the formation of the subject, he was also in full flight from phenomenology, existentialism, and the general "philosophy of consciousness" with which he might have produced an account of the everyday experience of surveillance. His emphasis instead was on macro-social factors; as a result, the issue of the experiential reality of surveillance is undertheorized in Foucault's writings and in surveillance studies that have followed in his wake.

In this chapter, we return to the overlooked question of the shaping of modern subjective experience through surveillance. We are not engaged in the polemics of Foucault's generation of French intellectuals for or against phenomenology and existentialism. Instead, we affirm the considerable heuristic value of phenomenology as a means of studying the subjectivity said to be produced through social and institutional structures and practices. We first address the issue of surveillance in an individual context and then consider the implications of our analysis for the institutionalization of surveillance in modern societies.

A phenomenological analysis first requires a return to the philosophy of consciousness rejected by Foucault. Such a return, however, implies a significant shift—some have termed it a "Copernican turn" (Husserl, 1937)—in conceptual vocabulary and methodology. This is a turn from social structures and processes described by Foucault to intersubjective experience, consciousness, and "intentionality" as described by Jean-Paul Sartre and Maurice Merleau-Ponty, among others.

The life of consciousness—cognitive life, the life of desire or perceptual life—is subtended by an 'intentional arc' which projects round about us our past, our future, our human setting, or physical, ideological and moral situation, or rather which results in our being situated in all these respects. (Merleau-Ponty, 1962, p. 136)

"Intentionality" refers to the projects, plans, and activities that fill and structure our everyday lives, and that similarly shape and orient commonplace awareness of the world around us. For Merleau-Ponty, intentionality is a kind of *a priori* that connects the individual to the lifeworld around her/him, structuring interaction, purpose, and meaning as they arise in everyday activity. The goal of the phenomenological method, as Merleau-Ponty explains, is to "loosen" this intentional shaping and structuring, to "slacken the intentional threads which attach us to the world and thus [bring] them to our notice" (Merleau-Ponty, 1962, p. xiii). In other words, the methodological goal of phenomenology is to make commonplace "microlevel" activities and the meanings associated with them objects of explicit reflection.

Instead of categorization and explanation, this approach requires observation and description, and even, at least at the outset, the explicit "bracketing" of theory and analysis. As Merleau-Ponty puts it, "it is a matter of describing, not explaining or analyzing" (Merleau-Ponty, 1962, p. viii). Instead of beginning with and articulating social formations in their institutional, macro-level dimensions, this method has as its starting point the intentional relationship that links the self to the concrete, everyday world around it. In this sense, phenomenology can represent, in Husserl's famous phrase, a return to the "things themselves" (2001, p. 2)

Phenomenological attention to the concrete, descriptive, and pre-theoretical is most effectively realized through the development of short narrative descriptions of incidents or anecdotes of everyday experiences (see van Manen, 1997). These descriptions do not appeal to a notion of statistical "representativeness" or generalizability. Instead, their validity derives from their being recognizable and compelling to their readers on a concrete, experiential level. This is accomplished through a process of writing and rewriting that bears some relationship to fictional composition—which, after all, must also be compelling and believable to readers. These accounts are initially developed through participation in and reflection on experiences that one undergoes oneself, or that are "experienced" vicariously or otherwise gleaned through unstructured interviews. One procedure among many that can be used in this research is "guided existential reflection" (van Manen, 2001), in which the researcher analyzes experience in terms of four themes: lived space, lived time, the lived body, and lived human relation (van Manen, 2001).

SARTRE'S "THE LOOK"

A phenomenological description that provides a starting point for our investigation of surveillance is provided by Jean-Paul Sartre in his famous passage on "the look" in *Being and Nothingness*. A short selection from this passage is excerpted below. It presents an especially clear analysis of the situation of observer and observed with which existential–phenomenological consideration of surveillance would logically begin.

> Let us imagine that moved by jealousy, curiosity, or vice I have just glued my ear to the door and looked through a keyhole. I am alone . . . behind that door a spectacle is presented as "to be seen," a conversation as "to be heard." The door, the keyhole are at once both instruments and obstacles; they are presented as "to be handled with care;" the keyhole is given as "to be looked through close by and a little to one side," etc. Hence from this moment "I do what I have to do." No transcending view comes to confer upon my acts the character of a *given* on which a judgment can be brought to bear. My consciousness sticks to my acts, it *is* my acts; and my acts are commanded only by the ends to be attained and by the instruments to be employed. My attitude, for example, has no "outside;" it is a pure process of relating the instrument (the keyhole) to the end to be attained (the spectacle to be seen), a pure mode of losing myself in the world, of causing myself to be drunk in by things as ink is by a blotter. . . . [. . .]

> But all of a sudden I hear footsteps in the hall. Someone is looking at me! What does this mean? It means that I am suddenly affected in my being and that essential modifications appear in my structure-modifications which I can apprehend and fix conceptually by means of the reflective *cogito*. First of all, I now exist as *myself* for my unreflective consciousness. It is this irruption of the self which has been most often described: I see *myself* because somebody sees me-as it is usually expressed. (Sartre, 1956, pp. 259–260; emphases in original)

The passage begins with a description of a hypothetical situation described from a first person perspective ("I have just glued my ear to the door and looked through a keyhole. I am alone," 1956, p. 259). This situation is, in a sense, a prototypical scenario of surveillance that is complete with the effacement or anonymity of the observer from the perspective of the observed that is characteristic of Bentham's panopticon and of other forms of surveillance.

Sartre characterizes this situation using verb phrases that are common in phenomenological analysis: Things are presented as "to be heard" and "to be seen." The door and keyhole are presented as "to be looked through close by and a little to one side." The point, as Sartre himself says, is to describe things not from an objective, impartial view (as if from nowhere), but rather, as they are tied up in our existence, projects, and intentions: "No transcending view comes to confer upon my acts the character of a *given* on which a judgment can be brought to bear" (Sartre, 1956, p. 259, emphasis in original). From the perspective of the person who would be spying, that is precisely how the door and keyhole appear: not in terms of their physical dimensions or material composition, but as an arrangement that can be looked through in a particular way in order to gain surreptitious access to what is said and done on the other side. But this entails special care and stealth, and the keyhole requires of the onlooker a specific and telling kneeling or bending posture. Sartre continues, arguing that in this surreptitious situation, his acts "are in no way known. [Instead] I *am my acts* . . . I am a pure consciousness *of* things, and things [are] caught up in the circuit of my selfness" (p. 259; emphasis in original).

Sartre's point is not that this observing self exists in solipsistic isolation, but that the self or consciousness is fully absorbed in the act of viewing and in the object of its gaze: "My attitude . . . has no 'outside'; it is a pure process of relating the instrument (the keyhole) to the end to be attained (the spectacle to be seen), a pure mode of losing myself in the world, of causing myself to be drunk in by things as ink is by a blotter" (Sartre, 1956, p. 259). Lived space, in this instance, is constituted solely by the space or the world observed through the keyhole. The lived body momentarily disappears, as the observer's intentional focus is absorbed wholly in what he is seeing and hearing on the other side. Lived relation is defined for a moment by the objectifying gaze of a hidden and anonymous observer, and by the people, actions, or objects observed on the other side.

But phenomenologically speaking, this is only half of the story. Sartre begins to explore the other half by introducing a kind of "eidetic variation," as it is called: A deliberate change is introduced in a particular aspect of the circumstances constituting the scenario or the larger lifeworld for the purposes of discovering how this aspect affects the configuration of meanings, projects and objects, and their interrelationship in that world: "But all of a sudden, I hear footsteps in the hall." By introducing the presence of another who is able to view the secretively observing self, Sartre is able to explore an entirely different ontological modality: "First of all, I now exist as myself for my unreflective consciousness. It is this irruption of the self which has been most often described [as follows]: I see myself because somebody sees me" (Sartre, 1956, p. 260). The self, earlier absorbed in the observation of others, now becomes itself the object of observation.

Being caught in the act of surreptitious surveillance, however, is not a matter of suddenly and simply "knowing" that someone is watching you; it is a change in one's way of being. The self is transformed from a subject to an object. It is no longer absorbed by what is being viewed through the keyhole; it becomes less of a subject or a consciousness, absorbed by the acts of others, and instead becomes an object, something fixed in the gaze of another. It experiences itself as seen through the eyes of the person who is viewing it. Lived space suddenly becomes the space of the hallway rather than the space on the other side of the keyhole. Lived relation is now largely determined by the objectifying gaze of a second observer. The lived body now becomes an object of acute awareness, and lived time is defined by anticipation of the response of the other.

Sartre's description also reveals a further aspect of the body that is significant for surveillance. This corporeal element is indicated in what Levinas referred to as the "autosignifying" function of the body in the gaze of another, and what Feenberg has called the "extended" body, manifest in forms of objectification such as signs and traces (1987, pp. 120, 112; Feenberg, 2006). This aspect is registered by the audible footsteps in the hall, and in the telling posture of the body of the observer at the keyhole. It is, in other words, the material aspect of the body that is perceived as meaningful by others, and indirectly by ourselves as well.

The audible footsteps and the posture at the keyhole, moreover, act as signals that go beyond the body's physical boundaries: They are the results of bodily presence that *indicate* a particular intention or consequence, but that are not tantamount to it: The observer at the keyhole may discover that the footsteps are those of an unconcerned child or a blind person; from the perspective of the person coming down the hall, the observer at the keyhole may well turn out to be a locksmith—someone looking *at* the keyhole, rather than through it. The significance of these "extensions" of the body, or of its various auto-significations is clearly contingent, depending on their interpretation and on the circumstances surrounding them. They do not precisely belong to our body and yet they are indices of our bodily presence that track us, and for which we can be held responsible. In today's world, they include the traces of DNA we shed as a natural organic function, and the automatic registration of movements, transactions, logins and downloads that increasingly accompany our everyday activities. As such, these aspects of the extended body provide new avenues for identification and control, as well as means for deception and resistance that are further explored in the next section.

THE BANK MACHINE

To pursue our own phenomenological investigation further, we have developed a written description, above, of an everyday experience of surveillance—that of using an ATM.

> As I enter the foyer where the bank machines are, I join the line up of people and wonder how long it will take me to make my withdrawal. As each person steps up to the bank machine and the line moves forward like clockwork, I notice whether someone takes extra time stuffing an envelope for a bill payment or a deposit, or whether someone makes multiple transactions. I notice how close the person behind me is standing to me. I clutch my purse a little bit tighter. Did I zip up all of my pockets on my backpack, I wonder? It is finally my turn to step up to the machine—to a stage where others will watch me as I have watched them. With an almost mechanical rapidity, I reach in to my purse and pull out my wallet, and pull out my bank card from its protective outer casing. I slide my card into the machine, and for a moment wonder if it will correctly read my card's information. I notice the person next to me taking longer than me to complete her transaction. I wonder why it appears like she's making herself at home in front of the bank machine. Leisurely putting down her things . . . and now she's answering her cell phone?! After I complete my withdrawal, I take my transaction record, read it once, and rip it up into tiny shreds that I quickly throw away. As I complete my turn and walk away from the machine, I look back to do a quick final check to make sure that I have not left anything behind of my transaction.

This description employs a number of techniques mentioned earlier—including existential reflection (on lived time, space, corporeality and relationality), interviewing, writing, and rewriting. Like many everyday scenarios of surveillance, this description presents characteristics that are more diffuse than in Sartre's ideal-typical description. However, many of the same themes and experiential elements remain salient.

In this description, the roles of observer and observed are both present. As in Sartre's passage, the two roles switch at a certain point, and the first-person observer becomes the observed as she steps up to complete her transactions at the bank machine. The characteristics established in the first part of the narrative are in many cases replaced by their opposites in the second. First, while in the lineup to use the ATM, relation, time, space and body are experienced as guarded waiting and watching, a careful awareness of self and above all of the other at the ATM machine. Time is dilated, filled with the impatient observation of the minutiae of others' activities. But when the narrator reaches the machine, the watcher becomes the watched, and is presumably being observed as she had earlier been observing others. Time is lived not as waiting but in terms of self-aware activity. Under the impatient gaze of the others (and presumably also of the camera embedded in the ATM itself), the lived body is experienced as objectified, as if on a stage before an impatient audience.

But unlike Sartre's account, at no point in this bank machine description is the consciousness of the observer completely and utterly absorbed in the observed, "as ink is by a blotter." The existential-relational quality of this situation, in other words, is not as purely objectifying as in Sartre's example: Those in the line and at the bank machine relate to each other not purely as anonymous, hidden observer and exposed observed. They are able to see each other, and have the potential to communicate in other ways. Similarly, after the observer steps up to the bank machine and becomes the observed, this change of roles is never absolute: She continues to observe, while also being acutely aware that she is the object of others' observation, and carefully monitoring her own behavior as a result of this awareness.

EXTENDED CORPOREAL TRACES AND PROXIMITY

An additional and indispensible experiential aspect of surveillance is one that is only indirectly registered in the description of the ATM line-up: This is composed of the silent recording and record-keeping functions of the ATM machine itself, the "minacious twinkle" in the camera's unblinking eye, as one surveillance studies text puts it (Lyon, 2001, p. 147). This takes us beyond the existential dynamics of the subject as perceiving and perceived, and even beyond explicitly intentional, thematizing and objectifying consciousness that was earlier described as one of the fundamentals of phenomenology. Here we are dealing with a feature of the environment, much like Foucault's example of the panopticon. And yet this environmental feature refers implicitly to an extended subjectivity correlated with the extended body of the surveilled individual.

The technical functions of the ATM that signify this ideal and sometimes real but always anonymous and invisible observer are not the object of explicit awareness of the narrator or of those around her. Instead, this is registered in what Levinas refers to as "proximity" or "a-thematic consciousness:"

> The immediacy of the sensible is an event of proximity and not of knowledge. . . . Proximity is not an intentionality. To be in the presence of something is not to open it to oneself, and aim at it thus disclosed, nor even to "fulfill" by intuition the "signitive thought" that aims at it and always ascribes a meaning to it which the subject bears in itself. (Levinas, 1987, pp. 116, 125)

A-thematic consciousness, in other words, is a type of awareness that is not intellectual, interpretive or deciphering. It is not one that centers around explicit meanings, themes, and significations—in which objectifying intention and consciousness would find themselves fulfilled. Instead, these meanings and themes remain implicit, mute and beyond conscious differentiation; they appear instead in the form of what phenomenological psychologist Eugene Gendlin calls "felt sense" and what other phenomenologists have referred to as "mood" or "atmosphere" (e.g., Heidegger, 1962; Schmitz, 1998). This felt sense is the result not only of the immediate situation, but also in the layering of (collective) memory and habit that contribute to a situation. Think of incidents captured by security and ATM cameras, accounts of petty crime and even identity theft associated with ATM spaces, transactions, and records. In the description given earlier, "atmosphere" or "mood" are not so much signified as they are indirectly communicated in the lived time, space, and relation arising from the strict, self-imposed monitoring and regulation of the narrator and of the others around her. This is the result not only of the immediate circumstances of the ATM situation itself, but of layerings of the mood it evokes.

This felt sense, mood, or atmosphere is also registered in the last sentence of the bank machine description, in which we read how the narrator takes her transaction record, rips "it up into tiny shreds," and disposes of it. This act has important implications both for a phenomenology of surveillance and for the issue of the "datadouble" or the "informaticized body" that has been raised by theorists of surveillance (e.g., van der Ploeg, 2003; Haggarty & Ericson, 2000; Mathiessen, 1997). Here the extended body is represented not only by the printed transaction receipt, but also by the coordinated provision of bank card and PIN code at the bank machine interface. Traces are in this sense aspects of our being through which we become objects in the world, but this is a process of which we are only vaguely, partially, or "athematically" aware. The customer at the bank machine conscientiously destroys the one trace she holds in her hand at the end of the transaction, but other traces have entered an infernal system of databases, networks, and hard drives from which they are unlikely to be wholly erased. This external and objectified self is functionally a doubling or simulacrum (Baudrillard, 1981, 1983) that can stand in for the person in all sorts of situations. We need only think of popular accounts of identity theft and error—such as individuals manifestly alive and well, but officially "terminated"— to recognize the reality of this doubling. Such doubling represents not only the trumping of the abstract over the concrete lived body, but also, of course, the objective, macro-social over the subjective and personal or of the system over the lifeworld (to use Habermas's [1984] famous distinction).

SUBJECTIVITY AND SURVEILLANCE STUDIES

Students of surveillance have been so impressed by the ever-growing completeness of this data image that they animate it as though it were an actual person. Identity is seen as coeval with an assemblage of traces rather than with actual presence. Thus, van der Ploeg writes of "the inability to distinguish between 'the body itself' and 'body information'" (van der Ploeg, 2003, p. 69). Haggerty and Ericson similarly write,

> the surveillance assemblage standardizes the capture of flesh/information flows of the human body. It is not so much immediately concerned with the direct physical relocation of the human body (although this may be an ultimate consequence), but with transforming the body into pure information, such that it can be rendered more mobile and comparable. (Haggerty & Ericson, 2000, p. 613)

There is something right about this turn in surveillance theory, and yet it is obvious that we are still able to distinguish the real person from the traces that person leaves behind.

The trace is bound to us by its origin and often by internal signs of various sorts, so we do not quite leave it behind after all. And yet we do not want to drag along every trace of our passage through life. We count on the erasure of most traces. It is this erasure that enables us to face the world afresh each day and to face it with a self-image we construct at least partially anew for each new situation in which we find ourselves.

In existential–phenomenological terms, privacy and secrecy are centrally constitutive of self and selfhood. Holding something private or secret emphasizes the difference between self and other, and confirms the autonomy of one's interiority and individuality. "Secrecy secures, so to speak, the possibility of a second world alongside of the obvious world," as Simmel (1906, p. 462) puts it. In contemporary conditions of surveillance and dataveillance, subjectivity itself is dependent on maintaining the gap between our embodied selves and our informaticized bodies. It would be intolerable for everyone to have full access to our salary, the details of our relations to our family, our medical histories, sexual proclivities, and so on. Such knowledge would completely objectify us and force us to live up to (or down to) the image of ourselves implied in this knowledge. Like Sartre's spy at the keyhole, himself espied, we would be evacuated of those aspects of identity and interiority concealed within us, frozen in the objectifying gaze of the other, and essentially deprived of our ability to function as a subject. We could no longer choose to project an identity appropriate to our inclination and situation as everything having to do with our identity would have been pre-empted. Truly, to be completely "outed" is to be annihilated.

However, while they suggest the devastating consequences of total exposure, the phenomenological accounts provided earlier also indicate a limit to the powers of surveillance. Along with the privacy and secrecy that are constitutive of selfhood and subjectivity come "negativity" and "transcendence," the fact that consciousness and the self are not just things in a predetermined social order. Part of the gap that separates the self from its data double is the fact that the double is a predictive tool, whereas the self that it ostensibly mirrors is capable of autonomous thought and action. As Majid Yar explains, in Foucauldian studies of surveillance,

> the subject of the gaze is rendered in terms of its *passivity*, confined to internalising the behavioural repertoires laid out by the disciplining authority. [These frameworks overlook] the extent to which the subject has an *active* role within its reception of the gaze, and renders it well nigh impossible to give an adequate account of creativity and resistance. (Yar 2003, p. 261)

Yar calls for a recognition of "the centrality of the consciousness of the subject" (2003, p. 261), and such a recognition, he argues, "opens the question of panoptic power to precisely the phenomenological question of *intentionality*, what the subject does or does not attend to in his relation to the world he encounters" (Yar, 2003, p. 261; emphasis in original). Our discussion has shown that our world includes the limitations imposed by the "traceability" of the observed, objective, and extended body, but also that these limitations are themselves qualified by their interpretable and manipulable character. This holds out a certain promise in the face of the proliferating powers of surveillance and dataveillance. Various stratagems of resistance are still possible. As Yar describes, these can range from the concerted efforts of groups such as the CCTV players to the strategies of those living (to a greater or lesser extent) "off the grid," as well as to those constructing and manipulating identities as hackers and thieves. Finally, as the events in Seattle in 1999 (and in other times and places since) show, the sheer, mobile, physical mass of political protests still poses a challenge to authority that is not easily controlled.

As these examples suggest, it is not the self and the body in isolation that present the greatest potential for resistance, but rather the aggregate effect of combined corporeal presence, working together in coordinated action. To return to our earlier example, Internet social activists such as those who use Facebook to organise activism, hacktivism or slacktivism, are vulnerable to being 'shut off' since they do not own the means of production of their communication (the country-registered Internet itself). This vulnerability, as well as other limitations in communication 'freedom', such as the ability of a government to also concoct profiles for the purposes of entrapment, was evident in the Arab Spring (2011) and according to many is an omnipresent condition for citizens of China (Zhang and Fleming, 2005). However, as the bank machine description indicated, it is through tacitly coordinated action in the spaces of awareness of the self and other which Michel Foucault called the "microphysics of power" rather than in his broader characterisation of dominant eras through genealogies that significant aspects of surveillance and the "enforcement" of social norms take place (Foucault, 1980,

1996; see also Paras, 2006). It follows that it is also in this collective space, and through different structures of collective awareness and action, that surveillance and the control it represents can be undermined and resisted.

To continue our recent example, according to some accounts, there had been sufficient prior online organising and consciousness raising for the Internet shut down in Egypt in February 2011 not to block the gradual amassing of successful pro-democracy (or anti-Mubarak) demonstrations. An indicator of success is the recent legal action against ex-President Mubarak for turning off the Internet. Social media sites such as Facebook can be employed to amass a quadrangle for a international pillowfight day (Bracken, 2011) or be mobilized in a city square to effectively delegitimize government. The platform's characteristics, limitations and affordances can serve as the basis for targeted marketing, allow for profile skewing for public opinion purposes, and enable new alignments and alliances for social action that materialize at the most unexpected junctures.

Our preliminary application of phenomenology to surveillance underscores and reveals a number of things. These include the importance of self-imposed constraints in relation to surveillance in our everyday lives as well as the significance of the objectification of the lived body in the recorded correlates of its physical manifestations. This objectification extends to the self or subject, but phenomenology simultaneously defines subjectivity in terms of its negativity, the private, unobjectified autonomy that subsists at its core, and that sustains the all important non-identity of the self from any informaticized *doppelgänger*.

NOTES

[1] The authors wish to acknowledge the support of the following grant in the development of this chapter: "Surveillance coping strategies and citizenship: From panopticon to synopticon," from the Social Sciences and Humanities Research Council of Canada/Standard Research Grants program file number 410-2004-769. Address correspondence to Norm Friesen, Canada Research Chair in E-Learning Practices, Thompson Rivers University, Box 3010, 900 McGill Rd., Kamloops, BC, V2C 5N3, Canada. E-mail: nfriesen@tru.ca.

REFERENCES

Baudrillard, J. (1981). *Simulacra and simulation.* (S, Faria Glaser, Trans.). Ann Arbor, MI: University of Michigan Press.
Baudrillard, J. (1983). *Simulations.* (P. Beitchman, Trans.). New York, NY: Semiotext(e).
Bracken, K. (2001). "The Urban Playground Movement." <<http://www.pillowfightday.com/>>. Accessed 02 May, 2011.
Feenberg, A. (2006). Active and passive bodies: Comments on Don Ihde's *Bodies in Technology.* In *Expanding phenomenology: A critical companion to Ihde*, ed. E. Selinger, pp. 189–196. Albany, NY: SUNY Press.
Foucault, M. (1977). *Discipline and punish: The birth of the prison.* New York: Pantheon Books.
Foucault, M. (1980). *Power/Knowledge. : Selected interviews and other writings, 1972–1977.* Reprint. New York, NY: Random House.
Foucault, M. (1996). *Foucault Live: Interviews, 1961–84.* 2nd edition. New York, NY: Semiotext(e).
Habermas, J. (1984). *Theory of communicative action: Reason and the rationalization of society, Vol. 1.* Boston: Beacon Press.

Haggerty, K. D., and Ericson, R. V. (2000). The surveillant assemblage. *British Journal of Sociology* 51:605–622.

Husserl, E. (1937). *The crisis of European science and transcendental phenomenology*. Evanston, IL: Northwestern University Press.

Husserl, E. (2001). *Logical Investigations, Vol. 1*. London: Routledge.

Levinas, E. (1987). *Collected philosophical papers.*.Dordrecht&Boston: Martinus Nijhoff.

Lyon, D. (2001). *Surveillance society: Monitoring everyday life*. Buckingham, UK: Open University Press.

Mathiesen, T. (1997). The viewer society: Michel Foucault's 'Panopticon' revisited. *Theoretical Criminology* 1:215–234.

Merleau-Ponty, M. (1962). *Phenomenology of perception*. London: Routledge.

Paras, E. (2006). *Foucault 2.0: Beyond Power and Knowledge*. New York, NY: Other Press.

Salt TV Network. (2011). "Hosni Mubarak Fined for Internet Shutdown." <<http://www. salttvnetwork.com/chapters/20110528/hosni-mubarak-fined-internet-shutdown>>. Accessed 28 May, 2011.

Sartre, J. P. (1956). *Being and nothingness: An essay on phenomenological ontology*. New York: Philosophical Library.

Schmitz, H. (1998). *System der Philosophie*. Bonn, Germany: Bouvier Verlag.

Simmel, G. (1907). The sociology of secrecy and of secret societies. *American Journal of Sociology* 11:441–498.

van der Ploeg, I. (2003). Biometrics and the body as information. In *Surveillance as social sorting: Privacy, risk and digital discrimination*, ed. D. Lyon, pp. 57–73. London: Routledge.

van Manen, M. (1990). *Researching lived experience: Human science for an action sensitive pedagogy*. London, ON: Althouse Press.

Yar, M. (2003). Panoptic power and the pathologisation of vision: Critical reflections on the foucauldian thesis. *Surveillance and Society* 1:254–271.

Zhang, E. and Fleming, K. (2005). "Examination of Characteristics of News Media under Censorship: A Content Analysis of Selected Chinese Newspapers' SARS Coverage" in *Asian Journal of Communication*. Volume 15, issue 3 2005, pp. 319–339.

MARIA BAKARDJIEVA

SUBACTIVISM

Lifeworld and Politics in the Age of the Internet

INTRODUCTION

Since the early years of its emergence the Internet has sparked curiosity, debates, and dreams revolving around its likely role in the reinvigoration of democracy. An area of lively scholarly debate on this topic has taken shape following the early speculations by pundits and futurists (see overviews by Feenberg, 2008; Friedland, 1996). Distinct schools of political theory have envisioned the democratizing potential of the Internet differently depending on the model of democracy informing their projections (Street, 1997; Dahlberg, 2001; Jenkins & Thorburn, 2003; Agre, 2002).

Cast in the categories of liberal individualism, both theorists and practitioners have anticipated and spearheaded projects that aim to realize direct democracy via elec as to transmit the vote of the individual citizen to centers of power through opinion polls and online referenda (Adonis & Mulgan, 1994; Dutton, 1999). Communitarian versions of democracy, for their part, have been excited by the community-building and -maintaining possibilities the Internet has opened up for local communities (Brants et al., 1996; Etzioni, 2003, Schuler, 1996). Active participation in community life online, this reasoning goes, will strengthen individuals' identification with common values and care for the common good. Besides the enhancement of local connectivity provided by community nets, or freenets, the Internet allows for networking between and among communities globally, introducing new opportunities for sharing and solidarity building.

The deliberative model of democracy that has at its core Habermas's notion of the public sphere—a social space where individuals come together as a public to engage in a rational-critical debate on issues of common concern—sees the Internet as offering new and more inclusive fora for public deliberation (Ess, 1996, Coleman & Gøtze, 2001). Recently, Dahlberg (2007) has given this perspective a radical-democratic slant by emphasizing the ways in which the Internet facilitates the emergence and growing visibility of "counter publics" composed of groups and interests that are not represented in the mainstream public discourses. What is characteristic of this "agonistic" public sphere is that it is driven by discursive struggle as opposed to a search for consensus. Examples of such counter publics are the Zapatistas movement, the antiglobalization movement, and other radical initiatives that cannot be inscribed in the mainstream public sphere.

Many of these visions have been informed by real-life developments. My goal here is not to question their validity or foresight, but to push at their limits. In this chapter, I

A. Feenberg and N. Friesen (eds.), (Re)Inventing the Internet: Critical Case Studies, 85–108.

would like to propose a perspective on the democratic potential of the Internet that casts light on facets of democracy located outside of the visible arena of politics, typically occupied by campaigning, voting, assemblies, and organized action in the street or the media. I would like to divert attention from the structural, institutional, and procedural effects of the Internet on democracy and direct it toward changes unfolding at the level of meaning and individual agency. My main preoccupation will be to inquire into the capacity of the Internet to enhance democracy through the multiplication and enrichment of the everyday practices of citizenship.

By definition, the citizen is the main agent of the democratic system. That is why a thorough elaboration of the different modes of becoming, being, and acting as a citizen is imperative for a valid model of democracy (Dahlgren, 2003). Voting, polling, deliberating, and joining in activist movements certainly represent key acts of citizenship, but they may not make up an exhaustive list. I share this hunch with a number of scholars who, in recent publications, have sought to expand the understanding of citizenship by introducing notions such as "civic culture" (Dahlgren, 2003, 2006), "cultural citizenship" (Hermes, 2006; Hermes & Dahlgren, 2006), and "public connection" (Couldry, 2006; Couldry et al., 2007). These are all attempts to grasp the political significance of those "fuzzy or ambiguous phenomena, grounded in civil society and the lifeworld, that fascinate empirical researchers," as Livingstone (2005, p. 32) has put it. A common feature of these works is the insistence that we should look for germs and projections of the political and public world in the private quarters and daily dealings of individual persons. Everyday thoughts, conversations, and activities have a bearing on democratic politics (see Couldry et al., 2007). Some of the necessary conditions for a functioning democracy exist at the level of lived experience, resources, and subjective dispositions (Dahlgren, 2003). Put together, these arguments mark a "cultural turn" (Dahlgren, 2003) in the study of democracy and political communication.

In order to define and distinguish the practices of *citizenship* from the numerous diverse practices comprising everyday life, I undertake a brief excursion into the theory of citizenship. What is citizenship and what are its practical manifestations? Where can they be found, observed, and understood? Due to the inextricable link between citizenship and politics, this involves an exploration of "the political." Is it a specific sphere of social life, a type of activity, or a relationship of a certain character and intensity? My next bout of definitional work deals with the everyday as a specific plane at which humans engage with the world. What is there to be gained from choosing to look for citizenship exactly on that plane? Can such an exploration help solve some of the intractable problems that have been plaguing attempts to trace citizenship across the public–private divide? I attempt to connect the problematic of citizenship with that of everyday life through the concept of *subactivism*. Subactivism in my definition is a kind of politics that unfolds at the level of subjective experience and is submerged in the flow of everyday life. It is constituted by small-scale, often individual, decisions and actions that have either a political or ethical frame of reference (or both) and are difficult to capture using the traditional tools with which political participation is measured. Subactivism is a refraction of the public political arena in the private and personal world. I then employ the concepts evolved in this theoretical investigation in the analysis of the data from an empirical study of Internet use.

MODELS OF CITIZENSHIP

Debates surrounding the notion of citizenship can be mapped out along several axes usefully outlined by Isin and Turner (2002). The long-standing liberal tradition has defined citizenship as a complex of unalienable rights and freedoms that individuals posses in equal measure in their capacity as members of a liberal-democratic state. Rooted in a set of formal rules, liberal citizenship has become a matter of status endowed on individuals automatically by birth or after a strictly regulated process of naturalization. The relationship between the social totality (the state) and the individual thus becomes an administrative relationship cast in the form of instrumental rationality: The state exists in order to secure favorable conditions for the individual's pursuit of his or her private interests and vice versa. The individual's main contribution to the state is in providing the means (through taxes) and performing the activities (observing the law, voting) that ensure the reproduction of the state. The citizen thus emerges as a client of the state and consumer of the protective and enabling services that it has to offer.

The communitarian view of citizenship, in contrast, endeavors to rescue a cultural dimension of citizenship that reaches more deeply into individual and group identity than the acceptance and abidance by a formally specified set of universal rights and obligations. In this view, community holds ontological primacy over the individual. Partaking in a moral and cultural agreement over shared values and meanings defines an individual's membership in a community. Instead of an emphasis on each individual's freedom to pursue his or her own good, communitarian thinkers insist on the centrality of the common good and ground citizenship in the act of its embracement and prioritization. The communitarian model overcomes liberal universalism through its attention to the social and cultural contexts of citizenship. At the same time, it idealizes the social uniformity and moral accord within communities.

A third model, the republican view of citizenship, is based on citizens' active participation in the republic, or the political community. The agency of citizens is one of the main tenets of this conception. In a republic, the governing of the state and society is a matter in which all citizens have to be involved. Republicanism has an expressed ethical dimension. It promotes "civic virtue," the ability of the individual to set aside his or her personal interests in the name of the public good. Republicanism does not discount individual interests and group or community belonging, but places the public as a political community at a higher level of significance. Citizenship thus acquires an integrative dimension: It is a "more general point of view" (Dagger, 2002, p. 150) from which the individual surveys his or her numerous interests, roles, and loyalties.

Critics of the republican model have focused their discontent on two main shortcomings. The first has to do with the fact that a public good is impossible to arrive at equitably in a complex society where numerous groups make conflicting demands reflecting their particular and often irreconcilable interests (Young, 1990; Mouffe, 1993). The concrete content of the public good is therefore an upshot of a hegemonic process in which dominant groups impose their meanings and will over subordinate groups. Another assumption of republicanism, that all individuals in a complex society are bound to acquire public virtue and skills for participation in self-governance, is an idealization that does not account for differences in access to resources, as well as economic and cultural inequalities. A third challenge that republicanism has had difficulty dealing with is the elusive boundary between the private and the public, the particular and the political, which incidentally represents a constitutive element of many of its central categories such as participation and civic virtue. Classical republicanism has extolled the public and put down the private, as in the sharp contrast the Greeks drew between the *polit'es*, the citizen playing an active part in public affairs, and the *idi'ot'es*, the private person who minded his own business and shunned the polis (see Dagger, 2002, p. 149). With a boundary so pointed and morally charged, the definition of the public as opposed to the private becomes a highly contested ground. Feminists, for one, have decried the low status ascribed to women under such a conception of citizenship and in some cases have advocated the recognition of the virtues of the private world and the extension of the notion of citizenship to include these virtues typically sustained by women. A much more interesting move, however, undertaken by feminist activists and scholars has been the one that calls for rethinking the very contrast or boundary between the public and the private as suggested by the formula "the personal is political" (see Hanisch, 1970, 2006). I will have more to say about this argument in the context of my examination of Internet use for civic purposes.

The theory of radical democracy engages the problems of republicanism head on. While retaining the ideal of active and equitable civic participation at its core, this theory subjects issues such as difference, inequality, domination, hegemony, and others to an incisive critical examination (Dahlgren, 2006). Its point of departure is an explicit attempt to draw on both liberalism and republicanism with a view to combining their insights in a new conception of citizenship (Mouffe, 1993, p. 62). Mouffe argues that "the recovery of a strong participatory idea of citizenship should not be made at the cost of sacrificing individual liberty" (p. 62). The challenge to civic republicanism, according to her, is to envision political community in a way that is compatible with modern democracy and liberal pluralism.

The theory of radical-democratic citizenship is suggestive for my investigation with its expressed effort to propose a reconstitution of the relationship between the public and the private, the political and the particular in a way that acknowledges the dynamics and complexity of both identity and politics in a late-modern society. Citizenship in this model is neither a paper certificate of entitlement, nor faithful abidance by community norms and values, nor selfless ascendance above private interests and concerns in the name of the common good. It is a special aspect of identity that meshes and interacts with all other facets making up who one is as a person. It is constantly in flux, open and susceptible to the social discourses in which the individual is immersed. Thus the main concepts on which this model of citizenship is based are those of *identity* and *"the political."* I examine them next in more detail, as they prove to be useful analytical tools in my further discussion.

IDENTITY AND SUBJECT POSITIONS

For Mouffe (1993), radical-democratic citizenship is a "form of political identity that consists of an identification with the political principles of modern pluralist democracy" (p. 83). She theorizes the individual "as a site constituted by an *ensemble of 'subject positions,'* inscribed in a multiplicity of social relations, the member of many communities and participant in a plurality of collective forms of identification" (p. 97). The subject positions, which the individual assumes, are themselves "constructed by a diversity of discourses among which there is no necessary relation, but rather a constant movement of overdetermination and displacement" (p. 77).

Subject positions emerge out of diverse social discourses and recognized social relationships. Identity is the upshot of the process of identification by the individual with a set of subject positions, a process that is ongoing and never completed. Identification, Stuart Hall (1996) maintains, is not lodged in stable commonalities and solidarities shared by members of "natural" groups. It is a "signifying practice" marked by contingency, involving "discursive work," operating through the "binding and marking of symbolic boundaries and the production of 'frontier effects'" (p. 3). It requires its "constitutive outside," difference, the other.

Hall offers several compelling observations regarding the workings of the process of identification. Identities, he believes, are "points of temporary attachment to the subject positions which discursive practices construct for us" (p. 6). Identities are produced by using the resources of history, language and culture in the "narrativization of the self" (p. 4). Although they include a strong fictional component, they possess high material and political effectiveness. Identification, Hall insists, is a two-way process. It involves the "hailing" or "interpellation" (a term introduced by Althusser) of the subject in a position crafted by ideology or hegemonic social discourses. It also requires an investment in the position on the part of the subject.

Positioning theory (Davies & Harre, 1990) represents a school of thought that has endeavored to examine the formative dynamics of subject positions at the level of interpersonal discursive practice. People construct their selfhood, these authors argue, by continuously positioning themselves in various points of the discursive repertoires provided by their culture and by speaking from those positions in the course of their daily life. However, "in speaking and acting from a position, people are bringing to the particular situation their history as a subjective being, that is the history of one who has been in multiple positions and engaged in different forms of discourse.... Such a being is not inevitably caught in the subject position that the particular narrative and the related discursive practices might seem to dictate." In this way, the notions of positioning and subject position improve on that of "role" employed in dramaturgical and functionalist sociological theory. A role presupposes lines already written for actors and a script determined by the particular play in which actors find themselves. Positioning and subject position, on the other hand, emphasize the improvisations and transformations actors introduce in the culturally established scripts by drawing on their own subjective lived histories with their attendant emotions and beliefs. Thus, it can be concluded, the "narrativization of the self" has two moving forces: the macro-discourses of power and the micro-discourses produced by subjects themselves amid the particular circumstances of their life situations and intersubjective experiences.

To fill a serious gap in the identity theories recounted so far, it is important to recognize that modern subject positions emerge not exclusively in the crucible of diverse social discourses, but also in the various points of complex institutional and technological networks (see Feenberg, 2009). These networks play a powerful role in the identification process because they influence to a large extent the access subjects have to social discourses of all kinds as both audiences and participants, as well as their direct experiences of the social world. A technological network based on the pulpit, the printed bible, and village word of mouth offers a substantively different set and scope of subject positions compared to a network based on the national newspaper or modern broadcasting technologies. The Internet transforms the process of identification by exploding the number of discourses and subject positions to which the individual becomes exposed, as well as by multiplying the participation forms available at that individual's fingertips. Moreover, by reaching deeply into users' everyday lives, Internet technology allows for active appropriation of discourses and constitution of new discursive repertoires by individuals and groups, thus bringing discursive agency closer to subjects' everyday experience.

Borrowing something from all these distinct takes on subject positions and individual identification with them, we can settle on a definition that recognizes the nonessentiality of identity and its constitution in social discourses involving power and authority (macro-discourses). At the same time, sufficient acknowledgment should be given to the constitutive role of the interpersonal and group micro-discursive practices in which an individual engages and chooses positions, as well as to the technological networks conditioning the access to and performance of these positions. In order to plug this concept into an elucidation of the nature of citizenship, however, it will be necessary to elaborate a criterion for identifying those subject positions that are more likely to make her/ him into an agent of the democratic polis. Subject positions are not political by default; however, positions that are considered apolitical at a certain point in time can turn into loci of conflict and antagonism and lead to political mobilization and new forms of struggle under different conditions and changed discursive dynamics.

THE POLITICAL: AN EXPANDING DOMAIN

Beck (1997) distinguishes three ways in which political science has operationalized its concept of politics: (1) the institutional constitution of the political community into which society organizes itself (polity); (2) the substance of political programs that shape social conditions (policy); and (3) the political conflict over power sharing and power positioning (politics). All these dimensions concern collective agents and their activities and interactions. Individuals are absent from this landscape of the political (p. 103). To this traditional view of the political, Beck juxtaposes a new one rooted in the processes of "individualization" characterizing "reflexive modernity." This view is captured in his concept of "subpolitics." Subpolitics represents a new mode of operation of the political, in which agents coming from outside the officially recognized political and corporate system appear on the stage of social design, including different professional groups and organizations, citizens' issue-centered initiatives and social movements, and finally, individuals (see p. 103). This vision introduces not only political actors organized around institutional and essential identities, but also collective agents of less comprehensive and permanent common characteristics and concerns. Isolated individuals are also mentioned as legitimate participants in this new game of politics. The world of politics, for Beck, is no longer that of "symbolically rich political institutions, but the world of often concealed everyday political practice" (p. 98). Individuals abandon the roles and allegiances handed down to them by custom and venture into constructing political causes and commitments of their own. They immigrate to "new niches of activity and identity."

Identity happens to be the central category around which Giddens's (1991) notion of the political in high-modern society revolves. The process in which Beck's individualized individuals "produce, stage and cobble together their biographies themselves" (p. 95) becomes the central playing field of politics in Giddens's view. Life politics has a generative, or substantive nature. It is a "politics of choice" as opposed to a struggle for the freedom to make choices. It is "politics of lifestyle," "politics of life decisions." It concerns "political issues which flow from the process of self-actualization in post-traditional contexts, where globalizing influences intrude deeply into the reflexive project of the self, and conversely where processes of self-realization influence global strategies" (p. 214). This politics tackles the question, "Who do I want to be?"

In his discussion, Giddens gives due credit to the feminist formula "the personal is the political," with which he connects the emergence of life politics as a dimension of the political in high modernity. The equation of the personal with the political, or more precisely the acknowledgment that issues considered to be strictly personal in fact have their roots and projections in the political sphere, has been one of the insights stemming form the Women's Liberation Movement of the 1970s. Carol Hanisch's essay "The Personal is Political" (1970) spelled out the dilemma that plagued women's discussions at that time regarding how to distinguish "therapy" from "political action." What were the issues that had to be confined to the personal sphere of women's lives and tackled within a narrow circle of friends and counselors, and what were the issues that the women's movement could confront in public as properly political? Hanisch is adamant that the discussions women had in small groups focusing on questions of their personal lives and beliefs were a form of political action. These discussions allowed the participating women to understand that they had to stop blaming themselves for the problems in their lives and to try to change the objective conditions in which their existence as women was framed.

The understanding of the personal as political has its heritage also in the work of social feminists like Elshtain (1998) who have been challenging the idea that the pub public, with its aura of nobleness, is the exclusive sphere of politics and citizenship. In the "small world," the world of private life identities are formed, moral qualities are nurtured, and resistance is put up to the oppressive forces and humiliating conditions experienced by some categories of individuals in the public realm. That is where the humanity of persons is reaffirmed and their dignity restored to them (see also hooks, 1992). Beyond questions of identity, matters of common, strictly political nature are also engaged and tackled with utmost seriousness within the small world. In her effort to find everyday-life contexts where public-spirited political conversations take place, Eliasoph (1998) comes to the conclusion that such conversations can more often be heard at the backstage, in private settings, than at public events or group meetings. While this finding comes as a disappointment in the ability of the different associations that Eliasoph studies to en-courage public-spirited discussion among members, it reaffirms the importance of the small world, as a site where individuals make sense of politics. Needless to say, the small world is also the place where media rep-resentations and discourses concerning issues of the political community are received, interpreted, and negotiated (Cruz & Lewis, 1994, Silverstone, 1994, Livingstone, 2005, Couldry et al., 2006).

This kind of redefining of the sphere and nature of the political carries some risks, as Mouffe (2005) has forcefully argued. It hides the danger of reverting the understanding of the political back to the narrowly individual choices and decisions where liberal notions of democracy and citizenship started out. The place and importance of collective entities in the constitution and operation of the political should not be overlooked, Mouffe insists. She criticizes the individualization theory put forward by Beck and Giddens inasmuch as it downplays and almost cancels the significance of collective identities for citizenship and political life in general. Beck and Giddens's version of politics, in Mouffe's view, turns a blind eye on power relations, hegemony, and the centrality of conflict and struggle to the political process. In her own way, Mouffe places identity and subject positions at the heart of the political, but for her not just any subject position or identity carries the marks of the political. Following political theorist Carl Schmitt, she asserts that the criterion of the political is the "friend–enemy" discrimination. "It deals with the formation of a 'we' as opposed to a 'they' and is always concerned with collective forms of identification" (p. 11). The political, then, is not a sphere of activity or a set of issues, but an ineradicable property of human social organization. Every religious, moral, economic, ethical, or technological controversy can transform itself into a political one "if it is sufficiently strong to group human beings according to friend and enemy" (Mouffe, 2005, p. 12). Feenberg (1995, 1999), for example, has shown how the interests of disenfranchised participants in technological systems such as medicine, telecommunication, and industrial society at large have gradually become articulated and have led to the emergence of politicized we-formations challenging the existing hierarchical order. With their collective as well as individual decisions and actions, patients with AIDS, Internet users, and environmentalists have clearly demonstrated that the technological can be political.

Building on the arguments recounted so far, I would like to distinguish three levels at which citizenship can be perceived albeit in quite distinct forms. The first two include the level of formal institutional politics and that of subpolitics as defined by Beck (1997). Note that as much as Beck emphasizes forms and manifestations of politics located underneath the surface of formal institutions, his construct retains a strong public and activist element. What seem to count as subpolitics are the organized and/or publicly traceable initiatives of social movements and individuals finding themselves in strategic points of the social system. The third level which I believe should be added to a comprehensive model of citizenship lies deeper under the surface than that. It could be referred to as the level of "subactivism." Subactivism is categorically submerged and subjective. It can be described as small-scale, often individual decisions and actions that have either a political or ethical frame of reference (or both) and remain submerged in everyday life.

Characteristic of subactivism is that its locus is the private sphere or the small social world. It blends ethics and politics, or oscillates around that fuzzy boundary where one merges into the other. It is rooted in the subject but necessarily involves collective identities often in an imagined form—recall Anderson's (1984) imagined communities. It is constituted by numerous acts of positioning—often in the imaginary vis-`a-vis large-scale political, moral, and cultural confrontations, but also with respect to ongoing micro interactions and conversations. It is not about political power in the strict sense, but about personal empowerment seen as the power of the subject to be the person that they want to be in accordance with his or her reflexively chosen moral and political standards. Its frames of reference are fluid and constantly shifting, responding to the ongoing dialogue between the subject and the cultural discourses permeating his or her social environment. The decisions and actions that constitute it have no permanent place in a person's agenda. They arise spontaneously, often as new dimensions of work, homemaking, parenting, entertainment. Subactivism may or may not leak out of the small social world and become publicly visible, meaning that its acts and products, although multiple, can remain insulated in the private sphere. This, however, does not condemn subactivism to inconsequentiality. The potential for it to be mobilized by trigger events and transformed into overt public activism is always in place. It is that essential bedrock against which individual citizens' capacity for participation in subpolitics or in the formal political institutions of the public world is shaped and nurtured.

Subactivism is best understood if the analysis starts from the point where the thinking and acting subject im-mediately experiences her physical and social world. The most productive route for performing such an analysis is charted by theories of everyday life and the lifeworld.[1] Lefebvre, for example, (1991) started his inquiry into the quotidian (everyday life) by distinguishing his approach from the preoccupation of philosophers and thinking people of his time with the political dramas acted out in "higher spheres" (p. 6), such as the state, parliament, or party policies. Lefebvre's interest focused on the "humble everyday base" (p. 6) of politics: in matters related to food, housing, rationing, wages, the organization and reorganization of labor. For him, everyday life was "what is left over after all distinct, superior, specialized, structured activities have been singled out by the analysis" (p. 97). It is the meeting place and common ground of all activities where the sum total of all relations that make the human being a whole takes shape (p. 97).

Among the numerous alienations plaguing everyday life, Lefebvre distinguished the alienation in political life, where the state takes on a power superior to the life of society. Traces of this kind of alienation can be sensed in the "I don't care about politics" retort by disenchanted citizens who have lost faith that anything they say or do can bring about any changes in the specialized and "superior" sphere of state politics. Indeed, modern society has circumscribed political activities in a specialized compartment, to which the ordinary person living his or her everyday life hardly has any access. The daily routines of work, housekeeping, childrearing, etc. erect an effective time–space barrier between the actual here and now of the ordinary person and the structured and highly profession-alized realm of political action. Nonspecialized political initiatives involving ordinary citizens require a rupture in the flow of daily activities and thus take a high investment of energy and mobilization work. The concept of subactivism is, I believe, useful in helping us conceive of a level of the political deeply embedded in everyday life. The very self-identification of the individual as an actor taking sides and choosing positions and courses of action vis-`avis debates and clashes of values and interests in a larger social world represents an elementary instance of subactivism. This self-identification could occur in the silent act of reading and interpreting political news as in the famous example of reading the newspaper in Anderson's (1984) treatise on nationalism. Or it could play out in the conversations around the dining table overheard by Eliasoph (1998). Or it can be taken out of the kitchen and put to work in the numerous frontier situations spanning the private and the semi-public such as neighborhood initiatives, school boards, etc.

Starting from a set of very different philosophical premises, Schutz sees the everyday lifeworld as "the region of reality in which man [sic] can engage himself and which he can change while he operates in it by means of his animate organism" (Schutz & Luckmann, 1973, p. 3). In this region man encounters other people (his "fellow men") with whom he communicatively constructs a shared world. These two features taken together make the everyday lifeworld "man's fundamental and paramount reality" (p. 3). A detailed exploration of the social structures of this experienced reality leads Schutz to map out an interlocking range of "zones of anonymity:" "The breadth of variations in my experience of the social world extends from the encounter with another man to vague attitudes, institutions, cultural structures and humanity in general (Schutz & Luckmann, 1973, p. 61). Between the immediately present "fellow man" and the abstract images of highly anonymous social collectivities and institutions stretches a continuous scale of "social typifications"[2] characterized by different "gradations of immediacy" (p. 69): of people the individual has met, but later lost from sight; of people or groups about which she has heard first-person accounts from her friends; of people and groups that she knows through myths and media; of social collectivities that she has been led to imagine indirectly and such that she finds even hard to envisage. The more remote and harder to reach and bring into immediate contact a social body is, the greater is its degree of anonymity.

Schutz's notions of actual, potential, restorable, and attainable reach hold particular importance in defining the capacity of the individual to come to know and get involved with the different personal and collective entities populating her social universe. These entities include friends, relatives, and family members, as they do cultural and professional groups, politicians, parties, civic organizations, governments, and nations. As I have argued elsewhere (Bakardjieva, 2005), this view of the experienced social world dissolves the dilemma of the public–private boundary. Instead of a duality of two distinct realms divided by a firm line, a multitude of intermediary states between the intimate and the highly abstract and anonymous emerges. Communication media with different affordances and the use genres they engender help individuals traverse this continuum and establish social engagements infinitely variable in closeness, content and intensity. The Internet has proven to be a particularly versatile vehicle for navigating the structures of the social world. My next goal will be to demonstrate the implications this has for citizenship. Thus, in what follows, I interpret the data from a qualitative study of home-based Internet use along the lines of the theoretical discussions and categories introduced so far.

THE INTERNET AND SUBACTIVISM

Methodology

The study was conducted in Calgary, Canada, one of the most Internet-saturated cities in a highly connected country. In-depth interviews were conducted with the members of 74 households between 2002 and 2004. Participants in the study were recruited by a variety of means, including advertisements in the local media and popular local web sites, interviewers' own social networks, and with the help of different local nongovernmental organizations (NGOs). The goal was to ensure that a wide variety of social categories of Internet users was included in the study. Diversity along socioeconomic and demographic lines was explicitly sought, but so was the presence in the sample of a set of specific life experiences such as immigration, disability, single parenthood, unemployment, and others, which were expected to shape Internet use in distinct ways. Although the prevalence of middle-class and upper-middle-class professional households in the sample could not be avoided, our explicit efforts led to the inclusion of a set of low-income families and individuals, as well as an assortment of respondents falling into the life-experience categories just detailed. In sum, the approach taken provided for a multiple and varied, albeit non-probability, sample of respondents and for rich data concerning numerous aspects of Internet use in everyday life

Altogether 192 individuals were interviewed about the purposes and patterns of their daily Internet use, 105 women and 87 men of various ages. The procedure took place in respondents' homes and consisted of a group interview with all members of the household, followed by individual sessions with each member who had agreed to participate, in front of the computer that he or she used to connect to the Internet. The declared focus of the study was Internet use at home. The inquiry followed several different themes, such as the history of the home Internet connection; Internet-related roles and rules; children and the Internet; Internet-supported activities; preferred information sources on the Internet; social networking and online group participation; and finally, reflections on the overall role and significance of the Internet in respondents' lives. Each theme was broken down into a series of probing questions in order to ensure consistency across the relatively large respondent group. At the same time, significant leverage was given to interviewers to allow respondents to recount their own "stories" related to each of the areas of interest in their own words and in a fairly open format. Questions concerning the political and civic uses of the medium were included in the package, but pursued only to the extent to which respondents felt comfortable answering them. One question asked respondents directly whether they had used the Internet for civic participation; other questions probed more generally into interviewees' perceptions of whether the Internet extended their "pos-sibilities for action in the world" and whether it made them feel "empowered." In a significant number of cases the interviewers had to decipher the notion of "civic participation" for respondents, which they did in ways and terms they thought appropriate to the particular individual and the context of the conversation thus far. Rather than being discouraged by this fact, I treat it as a finding and seek to understand what it tells us about participants' own understanding of the concept.

The quotes presented in this section have been selected from the data set due to their particular suggestiveness with respect to citizenship practices. Most of the authors of the statements quoted were people with higher education, while their occupations and current employment status varied. No quantification of the frequency of civic uses reported in the data has been made. Rather, the goal of the analysis has been to identify and categorize the various empirical manifestations of subactivism involving the Internet as they presented themselves in respondents' accounts.

What Is Civic Participation?

The direct question concerning civic participation produced three distinct types of responses: (1) an unconcealed puzzlement as to what this phrase meant, (2) some wild guesswork grappling at the meaning of the phrase, or (3) pointed and concrete accounts of forms of participation that entailed a "civic" quality in the view of the interviewed. Examples of engagement that could be qualified as civic propped up also under the rubrics of "action in the world" and community involvement, although they were not seen as belonging to the elevated and somewhat pretentious category of citizenship by respondents themselves.

Civic? Um, [long pause] I guess I'm not sure what the question means. I guess you know from the point of view of looking things up locally that might be going on or some-thing, yes I would do that. Um, like looking up whether there is a play in town or something like that?

Yeah. I was just checking out the [town's name] web site on Canada Day to find out what time the fireworks. And we didn't end up going down there, we sat right out here. School team registration.

Oh, hang on, there is one advocacy thing I've done just fairly recently, I haven't completed it. I'm filing a complaint with the Alberta College of Physicians and Surgeons.

Oh okay, I'm not into politics. I'm not apolitical person. I was married to one [laughs]. Didn't like it. You know... Actually I do do my taxes online.

As hesitant and off the point as these answers may sound to someone arriving from a serious theoretical journey into the concepts of the "civic" and the "political," they still betray an underlying liberal take on citizenship: The civic is related to services typically provided by institutional entities, be it the municipality, the school, the health care system, or the taxation office. Participation in this scheme of things is equivalent to consumption, compliance, or, at best, defending one's entitlement when it is somehow compromised. The Internet simply furnishes a smooth connection and extended reach to anonymous offices and administrative representatives or automated interfaces, whose anonymity is not reduced despite the engagement. It is a technical instrument in a formal process where roles and rules of interaction are inherited elements of the social structure. Citizens' positions in this relationship are given by default; they are enacted almost unreflexively, although it should be recognized that these positions require some enculturation and may not be automatically presumed by new immigrants, for example. There is hardly any aspect of these relations that can be defined as political. The waters have settled over imaginable debates and confrontations regarding the responsibility of the city to organize public celebrations, of the school to run sport teams, and of the public health care system to provide each citizen with an access to a personal physician. The "we" and "they" of this relationship is non-adversary as long as the "they" carries out its expected duties and provides the "we" with the services we believe we rightfully deserve.

Personal, Political, or In-Between: Spotting Subactivism in the Quotidian

Another type of answers to the "civic participation" question brings the action one step closer to the notions of conflict and active involvement. Notably, in the responses in this group, the civic retains expressed local and personal dimensions. It stems from projects and pragmatic interests originating in the immediately experienced social world.

Last year I was really involved in what we called the LEET process, which was the CBE's [Calgary School Board] ideas on how to decide which schools would be closed down. So each school had a parent volunteer. So you're very politically active. There's a lot of messages going back and forth between you and the Board, and the trustees, and the government of Alberta.... So yeah, I think it makes it easier because you have access to people that maybe you wouldn't have otherwise. (Lisa, 38, MSc. in genetics, stay-home mom)

It was actually my sister and I and a couple of other women had instituted this sort of fund raising group for Discovery House which is second stage housing here in Calgary for abused families, especially women and children but they have a program for abusive males as well. And so, we started up their main gala fundraiser and so we did that for three years and that was a way of communicating. And [then] I didn't have the e-mail or our computer for a lot of it, so I had to do it through my sister's office. But we still keep in touch, like, the group does, even though we haven't done it now for a year and like Discovery House will send us their stuff and what not. (Elizabeth, 43, social worker on disability)

There are several interesting things going on in these accounts: First, they are very close to home: The ob-ject of the activity is of personal significance to the women involved. Lisa has children attending a school that is among those under consideration for closing, while Elizabeth used to be a social worker with firsthand knowledge of the consequences of spousal abuse. Second, there is a directly accessible local organization that becomes the center of the activity. Third, a remote and anonymous dimension is also part of the package, as in the first case a set of municipal and governmental actors is the target of some of the action, while in the second, a dispersed population of potential donors has to be reached and convinced to contribute. Finally, a strong interpersonal component can be also detected. In the second case the respondent's sister and a group of women who had known each other before were part of the project. In the case of the school volunteering as well, Lisa had most likely known the school staff and other parent volunteers before she ventured into the process. The Internet comes in to facilitate both the interpersonal exchanges among "fellow women," and the reach into the previously unknown and faceless bureaucracy or circle of donors. It makes these activities more efficient and more feasible to the participants. More precisely speaking, the Internet helps furnish the critical leap between the closely personal and the anonymous and abstract, or, one may say, between the private concerns shared with friends and acquaintances and the public bodies necessary for any significant change to be affected. The intersubjective engagement with issues that already relate to or can eventually be bumped up into the public arena seems to be a crucial component of these respondents' civic involvement. Another woman described a similar chain of connections thus: "Some of my friends are involved in advocating for specialized things and looking at health care reforms and things like that, so I get a little bit involved in their exchanges" (Sonia, 52, physician).

In another example recounted by Elizabeth (see earlier discussion), the interweaving of the "private" and the "public" along with some halfway gradients of immediacy stands out even more clearly:

Like even with my mom who has Alzheimer's, she's in a long-term care facility. And my family's been really active in trying to have the government look at lack of funding and so, as I say, I e-mail my government about that, but there's also other sites I've gone into to look up information on longterm care facilities, like I'll go into specific care centers. I've looked up some of the qualifications they have for staff, the staff ratios. There's a couple of other organizations that you can get into, that are into these kinds of things, so in most of those things that I do, I do use it for those things. (Elizabeth, 43, social worker on disability)

In this case, an acute personal problem breaks out of the bubble of the private and particular small world and mutates into an issue demanding the attention and action of public agencies. With the help of the Internet, family conversations, web sites, advocacy organizations, and direct links to government representatives are entwined together and the personal is transformed into political in a very practical sense. This example demonstrates also how the formation of a collective "we" around the issue of care for Alzheimer's disease patients gradually progresses through interpersonal contacts, affiliations with organized groups, and finally confronting the government as the "they" that should recognize the deficiency and institute a change. It is indeed hard to qualify this particular instance of activism as political, as it does not contain the intensity of the we– they agonistic relation that Mouffe postulates. However, inasmuch as it refers to and targets established administrative and political institutions (the health care system, the government), it spills out of the social into the political, or at least has a strong potential to do so.

Submerged Activism: Engaging the Political Interpersonally

Answering the question "Has the Internet changed the way you see yourself in the world?" another woman engaged an issue of personal significance with expressed implications for minority groups in Canada and Canadian politics in general:

Fiona (56, lawyer): Oh for sure. There is no question. You know before—I mean..., now I am part of this. Before I knew something was going on out there. Now I am looking at those bills that they are, that [former Canadian Prime Minister] is trying to force through before he gets out. I am e-mailing people before he gets out. I am e-mailing people... I am lobbying the Alberta Government not to put a cap on pain and suffering at twenty-five hundred dollars which is absolutely ridiculous. I understand what they are trying to do. There are other ways of doing it. But to put a cap on it? But I am still lobbying. Which before I probably would have heard and said "oh, okay."

Interviewer: So the Internet has given you the potential to, I suppose, protest in a sense? Or is that the right word?

Fiona: Disseminate information. None of the people know until I tell them [about this].

Fiona is a lawyer of Aboriginal background. She consults different Aboriginal organizations on new legislation concerning Aboriginal rights. She does her own exploration of Government of Canada legal sites and takes a stance on the decisions and changes the Parliament plans to introduce.

From there on, she uses the Internet to spread the word, or as she puts it to "disseminate information" to the appropriate stakeholders, people like herself, who would be affected by the new legislation. By doing this, she actively constitutes a collective "we" capable of taking a position with respect to the changes: "I'm Aboriginal," Fiona says, "I want to know what *they*'re doing.... Now *they* want me to give up my privacy as far as my medical care goes in order to get medical care. And it's, if you don't do it, you don't get anything."

This type of activity is structured into Fiona's Internet browser and daily practice. She regularly reads and contributes to several online lists and groups that deal with Aboriginal legal issues and legal education. She has been the secretary of one of them and a representative on a few others. Her activism blends with her professional research and communication, but it is clearly distinguishable from a purely professional responsibility. Her self-positioning as a public Aboriginal intellectual is enacted through the micro-discourses and practices that the Internet supports and enhances.

Another professional with a civic mission, a graduate student in engineering originally from India, was intensely involved in collective we-formations that were totally virtual—his online groups. These groups had different but necessary input in his self-identity project.

The most useful thing on the web is having e-mail groups... I'm a member of more than seven-eight groups, on social perspectives and academics, social thinking, civic sense... They are Indian groups and they want to know my opinions, they read my letters.... Once, I did not write for a while, and I got a message from one of the group members asking how I was doing and worried that he hasn't seen my e-mails lately.... Whatever I'm writing about is in India... we have two thousand to three thousand contributors to these lists. I moderate a group called GIA, an e-group interested in geomatics. We don't have a very strong force back in India on geomatics. There are not too many students, but this allows us to chat, organize conferences, and exchange opinions and experience. We now have members from geomatics programs from all over the world. What we do is just align people on the same frequency, so to speak, bring them together, and focus on the same things. (Sami, 23, graduate student in engineering)

As this young man pursues his professional training, he is aligning himself with other professionals from his native country, thus building a stronger Indian geomatics "force." A distinct sense of belonging to a "we," both professional and civic, emanates from Sami's account. His own position and hence identity as a part of that collective "we" is reinforced through the recognition that the group gives to his presence and opinions. The "constitutive outside" of this Indian geomatics force seems to be the geomatics force of other countries in the world, against which the Indian network of scholars measures itself. There is no expressed agonism in this relationship, so it could hardly be construed as political, and yet a clear national and cultural frame of reference can be recognized. Needless to say, the Internet supplies the indispensable communication infrastructure through which this collective "we" becomes possible by connecting the actions performed in the everyday lifeworlds of numerous dispersed people.

A plethora of mundane collective we-formations lacking self-awareness as a civic force proliferate on the Internet, born in the group discourses of people sharing common interests, problems, and experiences. Cathy, a 51-year-old unemployed teacher, told the interviewer about the various newsgroups and lists she belonged to, especially stressing her "secular sobriety" forum:

> *Cathy:* Every kind of human condition, there's a group for it on Yahoo. So, you form your own little community regardless of where you live and exchange information that is supportive and it's monitored by the moderator and there was no messing around. It was a serious and very supportive bunch of people.

> *Interviewer:* What does the membership in these groups mean to you?

> *Cathy:* It was recovery, relationships, information, and strategy for growth.

> *Interviewer:* What do you mean by growth?

> *Cathy:* Growth just means I was in one place and now I am in another and the only difference is that group.

Another middle-aged woman, Esther, a 47-year-old farm wife, also spoke about personal growth in the context of her chronic illness, sometimes difficult life circumstances, enthusiasm for organic farming, and the online community she had created herself.

> So, I think the Internet has [pause] gosh [pause] I think I'd, in terms of personal growth I'd still be at the Neanderthal stage if it hadn't been for the contacts and the education and the opportunity that I've encountered online..... The time that I spend, I guess, some of us are able to donate money to charities, some of us are able to donate food to the food bank or clothing to the Sally-Ann or whatever. For me this is my 10%, this is, you know, this is how I give back to society even though it's an Internet community.

It would be a stretch to try to imbue such communities with any political implications. After all, they are just gatherings of private people willing to share their problems and lessons learned in specific situations of their lives. These are not the rational-critical deliberators of the Habermasian public sphere. The topics and issues they discuss are typically very personal, emotion-laden, sometimes social, but hardly ever are they perceived as political. At the same time, there is something paradoxical in displaying and trying to tackle such deeply personal problems in such public forums. There is a strange sense of empowerment in learning and being convinced over and over again that you are not alone in any, even the most peculiar, aspects of your personal life story and experience. For Esther, it felt like fulfilling a human duty (not civic, however, as she blanked out on the "civic participation" question) to extend her consolation and advice to people in trouble, to be, as she put it, "therapeutically productive" through her writing posted on her web site and in her online community. Forming such a bond, a small "we" preoccupied with a strictly personal, even if shared, agenda, certainly does not count much toward the global, structural, and/or institutional processes of government and decision making. I would nevertheless see it as a fragile form of subactivism, as it often involves taking a stance with respect to questions related to debates and clashes of a larger scale. Esther's abstractly humanitarian endeavor was tentatively framed by references to non-consumerism, sustainable agriculture, and alternative medicine, all denoting counter-mainstream values and action choices. She mentioned participating in a government agriculture-related web site where she would engage in exchanges with Canadian beef producers, telling them: "Well, if you're having to cut back on your beef production and sell your cattle, you know, maybe it's time to consider something different, something that isn't so hard on the planet, you know." Overall, the connections and interactions that the Internet supported for her made Esther feel better about herself, better than ever before, and that, she thought, was "very empowering."

In the examples of Cathy and Esther it appeared that a rather mundane and individualized form of life politics focused on the question "Who do I want to be?" was being actualized in the process of Internet use. Yet, recalling Mouffe's distinction between the social and the political, it isn't hard to imagine how such personal and, at best, social issues and preferences can be politicized in the larger public discourses and power struggles. Micro we-formations like the one created by Esther can become a resource to be mobilized and drawn upon. A joggers' group may turn out to be responsive to environmental issues, a pet-lover forum to calls for defense of animal rights, a parenting group to debates around day-care policies and funding (and ultimately, gender equity), the patient advocates to health care reform initiaitves,[3] etc. While not directly political, the groups in which these users negotiated and articulated their life challenges and choices constituted a subactive stratum of the polis, firmly embedded in the lifeworld, and yet quietly echoing categories of a broader political scope.

A Matter of Reach: Political Participation from the Living Room

In Miriam's experience the link between her personal moral and political choices and the institutional sphere of politics was much more direct but, interestingly, not mediated by a "we" collectivity. Miriam, a middle-aged woman disabled after a stroke, had used the Internet to run for an alderman position. This had been a life-political gesture in an important sense, as Miriam told us that despite her failure, she could now cross off this "thing" from the list of things she had wanted to do in her life. She saw city politics in very critical light, as "pompous pageantry" that hardly allowed for anything of value to be accomplished. She had decided to run for alderman led by her desire to change how things were done and possibly also to prove to herself that she was up to the task. The Internet had been her thoroughfare from her living room into the intricacies of city administration. She had used it to patiently educate herself about all this "crap" that she might have studied something about in school, but had completely forgotten:

> I got lots of demographics and information statistics from the different,... our city web site and then Alberta Government, you know, to just check statutes and all of that bylaw information and zoning and what's new, what studies have been done recently and all that. So it was very helpful for somebody that had never been involved in any political, you know ... I had to start somewhere; it was a good place to start. Then I also got how to write a campaign plan. I got the whole, mostly United States [material]. That, I tell you, they have got some excellent ideas. So that helped me formulate my campaign, so I became my own campaign manager and then there's a whole bunch of steps to follow in between. I can tell you why I didn't succeed—I didn't have any money. So, you know, I did learn a lot and it was a very valuable exercise for me....I might be able to offer assistance to somebody else because I have stored all of those web sites and information and everything I did in my campaign.

A 37-year-old medical scientist, Gregory, had used the direct thoroughfare into the institutional sphere of politics in a different, not quite so engaged and yet personally meaningful fashion. He was a man of a more cosmopolitan orientation and cared passionately about political events happening around the world. The Internet was his source of quality information about world politics, as he did not think he could rely on traditional media for that. He had fastidiously selected the sources that he drew on to keep abreast of developments: Listening to BBC radio on his computer at breakfast was part of his morning routine; he regularly researched the "superb" archives of the NPR, a public radio station in the United States, that he said he was "very fond of;" his highly customized Yahoo! page supplied him with the daily news from Reuters:

> It's just the thing, being able to listen to the BBC news. I really enjoy that news. CNN... we never would think about going that route. It's a sexy kind of over-dramatized and totally one-sided..., in so many instances it kills me. And the BBC just seems so fair in comparison.

Naturally, Gregory held opinions based on this information that he considered solid and well thought out. So, in a complementary move, he would occasionally write to the Prime Minister of Canada when a Canadian position with respect to international developments had to be worked out. Gregory talked about this as a kind of civic involvement, albeit with a trace of disenchantment in his voice: "Well, I write a letter to our Prime Minister—probably three times a year [chuckles]. I haven't got a meaningful response yet. But I keep on writing. This is particularly surrounding my own feelings, surrounding the war in Iraq and the way I see our place in the world and just wanting him to know one Albertan's opinion." Gregory was grateful to e-mail for allowing him to do something like that fast, without much complication, and saw it as an enlargement of his possibilities for action in the world:

> Writing a letter to the Prime Minister of Canada would be something that I would never do. Firing off an e-mail, which takes me 30 minutes to write, a really nice e-mail—it's a relaxing thing to do and I know it gets there right away—boom, I can forget about it.

Besides this direct personal expression of opinion, he had been part of the mailing list of a local anti-Iraqi-sanctions group, hoping "to make my point known in Ottawa ... I was asking for the sanctions to be broken because of humanitarian reasons, not military." The invasion of Iraq, however, had dampened Gregory's enthusiasm for participating because, he said, "things are out of my hands now."

Gregory's case to me is an excellent illustration of what it looks like to take a subject position vis-à-vis discourses circulating in the public world. Gregory invested a substantial amount of work in selecting and formulating his position and subsequently took that position very seriously. Undertaking steps to make his point known in Ottawa, individually and through the mediation of a micro we-formation, was an action following from his chosen subject position of a sanctions opponent and war - opponent. His determination in performing this action was frail for sure, as his rather disheartened response and recoil following the invasion of Iraq demonstrate. Nevertheless, short of marching down the street, his civic engagement is very obvious in his daily activities and choices. These activities and choices are certainly molded by the sources of information and discussion to which he has access, but Gregory navigates these sources in a very mindful and selective manner. These activities and choices are also circumscribed by the cultural resources and the time that the individual can commit to them. Note Gregory's insistence on the importance of speed and ease as factors facilitating his actions. His remarks resonate with participants' accounts quoted earlier that also hinged on ease, speed, and scope of e-mail communication with virtual and actual group members and institutions. As much as these may appear obvious and banal details, they do matter a lot in the materialization of the tiny gestures that subactivism consists of. By affording ease, speed, and scope, the Internet brings the otherwise remote and anonymous political bodies within attainable reach. It makes civic participation, not as a specialized activity in a superior (public) sphere, but as a concrete action amid everyday life, more practically feasible.

Here is probably the right place to make it clear that I do not think of the Internet as producing or setting off sub-activism. I agree with Agre (2002) that the Internet rather amplifies existing impulses and forces. Yet I consider it important to change the grammatical subject in statements like that. It is users who appropriate the technical functionalities of the Internet to position themselves with respect to discourses of different scale and character and to take action concordant with their emerging and changing subject positions. In the process, they weave together discourses and actions unfolding at the levels of the personal, interpersonal, small group, quasi-formal organization, public body, and institution in new ways. Thus, numerous new forms of subactivism evolve around the Internet with added capacity to traverse effectively the private–public continuum and make civic engagement more deeply embedded in everyday life. Internet-aided subactivism can be seen as a prime example of the "democratic rationalization" of the Internet itself (Feenberg, 1999, 2009). It is an ensemble of diverse sociotechnical practices generated by ordinary users that blend new technology and citizenship in unexpected ways. These are not the forms of civic and political use of the technology envisaged within the rationality of political and technological elites. These are rational choices emerging out of lifeworlds whose structures have been poorly understood or ignored.

CONCLUSION

Going back to the various readings of the incipient relationship between the Internet and democracy, I would like to throw subactivism into the mix. We may not be seeing an automatic rise in informed decision making by rational-born citizens knowing their best interests, as the liberal view would have it. We do not observe massive growth of solidarity and consensus over the nature of the public good as communitarians may have hoped. Disappointingly, the spread of forums and competencies for rational-critical debate on issues of common interest has not been as wide as the deliberative model advocates would have liked.

A recapitulation made from a different angle, that of the loci of politics, shows that public institutions have poured ample resources and scored positive results in harnessing the Internet in the service of state administrations and political bodies. Even though these advancements have contributed to more fluid institution–citizen transactions, the majority of them have been organized around the provider–client paradigm, ensuring better service, but extraneous to political democracy. Subpolitical players (as defined by Beck, 1997), for their part, have thrived on the possibilities introduced by the Internet to create counter-publics, to focus the attention and coordinate the actions of dispersed and transient collectives. It is a pity that their spirited and deserving causes have often remained unheeded and unsupported by the apathetic masses of the general population. Finally, turning to these ill-reputed apathetic masses, all one can find, and it takes very dedicated looking, is subactivism—feeble motions immersed in the everyday many times removed from the hot arena of politics. For these motions of personal positioning and weaving of connections across erstwhile zones of anonymity the Internet has proven a real blessing, but their consequences have been neither revolutionary, nor even conspicuous.

So then, has the Internet contributed in any way to the growth of democracy and does it hold any promise for such a contribution? The answer, and the potential of the medium, I believe, does not lie at any of these levels taken separately, but in the possibility for their interweaving. My insistence in this chapter has been that first of all sub-activism has to be recognized as an important dimension of democracy grounded in individuals' paramount reality, the point where they are capable of gearing into the world through talk, deed and interaction. This province of democracy will remain closed off and largely inconsequential to the affairs of the polis, if no proper bridges are built between it and the subpolitical and strictly political strata populated by collectives, organizations and institutions. So, I suppose, the central question to ask becomes: What are these proper bridges? What do they look like? Who are their prospective engineers and builders? Attempts have been made to construe such bridges as a form of marketing and public relations (see Bennett, 1998). I am wary of this approach, as it has proven to lead no further than the provider-client model. New formats of *interactive civic relations* are necessary designed to capture and channel the powers of the Internet to the benefit of a thoroughgoing democracy. The first and critical step down that road is the acknowledgment and orientation to subactivism as a major reservoir of civic energy. Perhaps movement activists and issue activists should start by recalling the wisdom of the brilliant short essay that put the phrase "the personal is political" on the conceptual map—just replace "women" by "citizens" in this quote:

> I think "apolitical" women are not in the movement for very good reasons, and as long as we say "you have to think like us and live like us to join the charmed circle," we will fail. What I am trying to say is that there are things in the consciousness of "apolitical" women (I find them very political) that are as valid as any political consciousness we think we have. (Hanisch, 1970, p. 5)

There are also, I argue, things in the Internet-use practices of "apolitical" citizens that are a valid indication of how the construction of a democratic Internet and of a thoroughgoing democracy can enhance one another.

NOTES

[1] For a more detailed discussion of theories of everyday life and their relevance to Internet studies, see Bakardjieva (2005).

[2] Typifications, in Schutz's language, are aggregate and abstract perceptions of objects and social entities in the lifeworld that lie outside of an individual's immediate here and now, i.e., out of her zone of "actual reach."

[3] Mentions of participation in all these kinds of online groups appeared in the data set from the 74 households studied.

REFERENCES.

Agre, P. 2002. Real-time politics: The Internet and the political process. *The Information Society* 18:311–331

Adonis, A., and G. Mulgan. 1994. Back to Greece: The scope for direct democracy. *Demos Quarterly* 3:2–9.

Bakardjieva, M. 2005. *Internet society: The Internet in everyday life.* London: Sage.

Brants, K., M. Huizenga, and R. van Meerten.1996. The new canals of Amsterdam: An exercise in local electronic democracy. *Media, Culture and Society* 18(2):233–248.

Beck, U. 1997. *The reinvention ofpolitics: Rethinking modernity in the global social order.* Cambridge, UK: Polity Press.

Bennett, L. W. 1998. The uncivic culture: Communication, identity, and the rise of lifestyle politics. *PS: Political Science & Politics* 31(4):741–761.

Coleman, S., and J. Gøtze. 2001. *Bowling together: Online public engagement in policy deliberation.* London: Hansard Society. http://www.bowlingtogether.net. (accessed: September 22, 2008).

Couldry, N. 2006. Culture and citizenship: The missing link? *European Journal of Cultural Studies* 9(3):321–339.

Couldry N., S. Livingstone, and T. Markham. 2007. Connection or disconnection? Tracking the mediated public sphere in everyday life. In *Media and public spheres,* ed. R. Butsch, pp. 28–42. New York: Palgrave-Macmillan.

Cruz, J., and J. Lewis. 1994. *Viewing, reading, listening: Audiences and cultural reception.* Boulder, CO: Westview Press.

Dagger, R. 2002. Republican citizenship. In *Handbook of citizenship studies,* eds. E. Isin and B. Turner, pp. 145–157. London: Sage.

Dahlberg, L. 2001. Democracy via cyberspace: Examining the rhetorics and practices of three prominent camps *New Media & Society* 3(2):187–207.

Dahlberg, L. 2007. The Internet and discursive exclusion: From deliberative to agonistic public sphere theory. In *Radical democracy and the Internet: Interrogating theory and practice,* eds. L. Dahlberg, and E. Siapera, pp. 128–147. London: Palgrave.

Dahlgren, Peter. 2003. Reconfiguring civic culture in the new media milieu. In *Media and political style: Essays on representation and civic culture,* eds. J. Corner, and D. Pels, pp. 151–170. London: Sage.

Dahlgren, P. 2005. The Internet, public spheres, and political communication: Dispersion and deliberation. *Political Communication* 22:147–162.

Dahlgren, Peter. 2006. Doing citizenship: The cultural origins of civic agency in the public sphere. *European Journal of Cultural Studies* 9(3):267–286.

Dahlgren, P. 2007. Civic identity and net activism: The frame of radical democracy. In *Radical democracy and the Internet,* eds. L. Dahlberg, and E. Siapera, pp. 55–72. London: Palgrave Macmillan.

Davies, B., and R. Harr´e. 1990. Positioning: The discursive production of selves. *Journal for the Theory of Social Behavior* 20(1): 43–63. Reprinted with modifications as chaper 3 in *Positioning Theory: Moral Contexts of Intentional Action,* eds. Rom Harr´e and Luk van Langenhove. Malden, MA: Blackwell. http://www.massey. ac.nz/~alock/position/position.htm (accessed December 1, 2008).

Eliasoph, Nina. 1998. *Avoiding politics: How Americans produce apathy in everyday life.* Cambridge, UK: Cambridge University Press.

Elstein, J. B. 1998. Antigone's daughters. In *Feminism and politics,* ed. A. Phillips, pp. 363–377. Oxford, UK: Oxford University Press.

Etzioni, A. 2003. Are virtual and democratic communities feasible? In *Democracy and new media,* eds. H. Jenkins, and D. Thorburn, pp. 85–100. Cambridge, MA: MIT Press.

Ess, C. 1996. The political computer: Democracy, CMC and Habermas. In *Philosophical perspectives on computer-mediated communication,* ed. C. Ess, pp. 197–230. Albany, NY: State University of New York Press.

Feenberg, A. 1995. *Alternative modernity: The technical turn in philosophy and social theory.* Los Angeles: University of California Press.

Feenberg, A. 1999. *Questioning technology.* New York: Routledge. Feenberg, A. 2009. Critical theory of communication technology: Introduction to the special issue. *The Information Society,* this issue.

Friedland, L. 1996. Electronic democracy and the new citizenship. *Media, Culture and Society* 18:185–212.

Giddens, A. 1991. *Modenity and self-identity: Self and society in the late modern age*. Stanford, CA: Stanford University Press.

Hall, Stuart. 1996. Introduction: Who needs "identity?" In *Questionsof cultural identity*, eds. Stuard Hall and Paul du Gay, pp. 1–17. London: Sage.

Hanisch, C. 1970. The personal is political. In *Notes from the second year: Women's liberation*, eds. S. Firestone, and A. Koedt. http:// scholar.alexanderstreet.com/download/attachments/2259/Personal+ Is+Pol.pdf?version=1 (accessed December 1, 2008).

Hermes, J., and P. Dahlgren. 2006. Cultural studies and citizenship. *European Journal of Cultural Studies* 9(3):259–265.

hooks, bell. 1990. *Yearning*. Boston: South End Press.

Isin, E., and B. Turner. 2002. *Handbook of citizenship studies*. London: Sage.

Jenkins, H., and D. Thorburn. 2003. *Democracy and new media*. Cambridge, MA: MIT Press.

Jenkins, H., and D. Thorburn., 2003. Introduction: The digital revolution, the informed citizen and the culture of democracy. In *Democracy and new media*, eds. H. Jenkins and D. Thorburn, pp. 1–17. Cambridge, MA: MIT Press.

Livingstone, S. 2005. On the relation between audiences and publics. In *Audiences and publics: When cultural engagement matters for the public sphere*, ed. S. Livingstone, pp. 17–42. Bristol, UK: Intellect Press.

Lefebvre, Henri. 1971. *Everyday life in the modern world*. New York: Harper & Row.

Lefebvre, Henri. 1991. *Critique of everyday life, Vol. 1: Introduction*. New York: Verso.

Mouffe, Chantal. 1993. *The return of the political*. London: Verso. Mouffe, Chantal. 2005. *On the political*. London: Routledge.

Schuler, D. 1996. *New community networks: Wired for change*. Reading, MA: Addison-Wesley.

Schutz, Alfred, and Luckmann, T. 1973. *The structures of the life-world*. Evanston, IL: Northwestern University Press.

Silverstone, Roger. 1994. *Television and everyday life*. New York: Rout-ledge.

Street, J. 1997. Remote control? Politics, technology and 'electronic democracy.' *European Journal of Communication* 12(1): 27–42.

Young, I. M. 1990. *Justice and the politics of difference*. Princeton, NJ: Princeton University Press

KATE MILBERRY

HACKING FOR SOCIAL JUSTICE

The Politics of Prefigurative Technology

INTRODUCTION

Since the eruption of the global justice movement at 1999's Battle of Seattle, much
has been said about the impact of the Internet on progressive activism. Of
particular interest have been the ways in which activists have used the Internet as a
communication medium. Cyberactivism—political activism on the Internet - is a
new mode of radical action, and novel practices such as virtual sit-ins, online petitions
and email campaigns have enlarged the repertoire of contestation (McCaughey &
Ayers 2003).

Activists in the global justice movement (GJM) have embraced digital
communication technologies in their struggle against the ramifications of global
capitalism. Indeed, the Internet has played an unprecedented role in the way this
movement has organized, mobilized, and disseminated information, enabling it to
emerge as a globally networked force for progressive social change[1] Distinct from
the hierarchical, labor-based social movements of the early 20th century, or the
'new social movements' that emerged from the countercultural revolution of the
1960s, the "newest social movements" (Day, 2005) are nodal, networked and
leaderless. Described as a 'movement of movements,' (Klein, 2004) the newest
social movements organize across social and geographical bounds, based on
affinity and a general critique of the ill effects of neoliberalism. They organize
daily against ongoing injustice in their local communities, and come together
temporarily and occasionally for large manifestations against globalized capital,
mobilizing via digital and mobile communication networks. In the late 1990s and
early 2000s, combination of interactive digital technology and activism was novel.
It was facilitated by 'tech activists'—programmers, coders, and hackers who
subscribe to the philosophy of the free software movement and are committed to
the pursuit of social justice. They are responsible for the design of the digital
infrastructure used by activist groups to advance movement goals.

But these self-described geeks do more than building and maintaining websites,
wikis, email accounts and mailing lists, and providing technical support. They also
customize software to meet the needs of activists engaged in the GJM. This new
brand of activism goes beyond simply using technology toward particular ends to
include the modification and transformation of technology itself. In developing and
deploying software that supports the realization of a virtual public sphere in
cyberspace, tech activists are enhancing the democratic potential of the Internet.

A. Feenberg and N. Friesen (eds.), (Re)Inventing the Internet: Critical Case Studies, 109–130.

Their work, therefore, is altering not only the way people 'do' activism, as many scholars have noted; it is also changing the face of the Internet itself.

The novelty of tech activism lies in the way tech activists incorporate the democratic goals of the global justice movement into the very technology used to pursue those goals. Tech activists recode software in a way that anticipates the progressive social change its users pursue; in this way, their theory of social change begins in practice. Thus tech activists produce both an alternative version of the technology that is accessible, participatory, cooperative and non-hierarchical, and an alternative vision of society based on those same ideals. In turn, their democratic interventions into technological development enable communicative practices oriented toward freedom and equality offline.

This chapter traces the rise of tech activism, which has roots in the free software movement but has cultivated its own ethically grounded and socially informed agenda. It examines how and why tech activists have appropriated wiki technology, using it as a space and tool for democratic communication in cyberspace. It shows how this, in turn, has enabled the realization of new communicative practices offline, establishing a dialectical relation between the technological and the social. Democratic practice online prefigures the possibility of a more just society. Actualized as democratic interventions into the development and use of technology, it manifests in alternative modes of social organization in the 'real' world.

INVENTING THE INTERNET

Detailed histories of the Internet reveal the socially contingent nature of its technical development (Abbate 1999; Ceruzzi 2003). The Internet is not simply the culmination of the long march of technological progress, but came into existence through a process very much informed by social factors. By considering the Internet's lineage through a critical constructivist lens, we can better understand how the goals and values of the global justice movement are inflected in the Internet's ongoing 'invention' (Abbate).

Initially conceived as a means for connecting government researchers at various military and academic institutions, the Internet was designed to enable the sharing of expensive computing resources (Hafner & Lyon 1996). According to Abbate (1999), the early Internet "favored military values, such as survivability, flexibility, and high performance, over commercial goals, such as low cost, simplicity, or consumer appeal" (p. 5). From its inception the Internet was designed to be robust, versatile and the responsive to unforeseen user demands.

The designers of ARPANET—the progenitor of the Internet—were also first generation users, and as such, they intervened in the design process in ways that strayed from the official vision of military computer networking. Imagined as a device for information dissemination and resource sharing, early Internet technology was appropriated and redeployed by users for purposes that differed from official expectations. Feenberg and Bakardjieva (2004) call this "creative appropriation" wherein "users innovate new functionalities for already existing technologies" (p. 16). Unexpected user-developed applications such as electronic mail, the Bulletin Board System and Usenet groups are all examples of this (Edwards 2003).

However, these applications do not reflect the hegemonic values of the ruling elite—values that typically inform and constrain technical development in modern industrial society. For example, neither the norms of corporate capitalism, such as exclusivity, profit, competition, scarcity and inequality, nor those of the military including secrecy, hierarchy, and centralized control, favor the sort of free communication that has emerged on the Internet. Features of its architecture intended to protect it in case of attack turn out to undermine these norms. The Internet is characterized by openness in its standards, its engineering and its software, and its early development relied upon values such as such as voluntarism, cooperation, sharing and collaboration. Despite its near total commercialization the ongoing evolution of the Internet remains dependent on values such as accessibility, decentralization and inter-operability. This has led many enthusiasts to hail the Internet as an inherently democratic medium (Rheingold 1993; Tidwell 1999). Others, it should be noted, insist the Internet is just the latest in the long line of communication technologies serving the system (McChesney 1999). The reality likely lies somewhere in between.

THE TECHNICAL CODE OF THE INTERNET

The Internet is an unfinished and flexible technology (Feenberg & Bakardjieva 2004). Conflicts over its design and meaning have not been resolved: will it become a cybermall dedicated to consumption, or a virtual public sphere capable of enhancing democracy? Considered from another angle, will the Internet develop along a path that leads to stability through imposing constraints, or will its generative nature—"the essential quality animating the trajectory of information technology innovation" (Zittrain 2006, p. 1980)—prevail? Clearly, the Internet has not reached closure in the design process and as such, has not yet been entirely encoded with the dominant norms.

The concept of the 'technical code' refers to the values and concerns that prevail in the design process, and are materialized in the technology itself (Feenberg 1995). The technical code of panoptic prisons, for example, embodies social norms of surveillance, self-discipline, and control. Winner (1986) observes how early 20th century building codes reflected and maintained the marginalization of handicapped people.

In western neoliberalism, the dominant norms and values are those of capitalism: exclusivity, profit, competition, scarcity, individualism and inequality comprise an array of 'unexamined cultural assumptions' that directly reflect the dominant social order. Because such values - products of the prevailing economic and social interests - are "literally designed into the technology itself" (p. 87), they appear as a technical requirement. This, however, is nothing but ideological sleight of hand; when the technological design process is historicized, the social origins of the technical code are made apparent. Technology, on this account, can never be neutral; rather it tends to reinforce and reproduce prevailing socio-economic power structures.

The concept of the technical code is important as an alternative to the notion of technological imperatives. This latter holds that technological development is evolutionary and inevitable, and that it must, in teleological fashion, be accepted as a desirable social advance, albeit one out of human control. In sharp contrast, conceiving of technological development in terms of the technical code brings to light both technology's contingent nature and the concomitant potential for human agency. This contingency reveals an opening in the design process for what Feenberg (2002) calls democratic rationalization of technology. "Democratic rationalizations challenge harmful consequences, undemocratic power structures, and barriers to communication rooted in technological design" (p. 16). In other words, democratic rationalization is the means by those most affected by technology – users—gain some agency in its creation. User interventions at the levels of use *and* design can alter technical codes, and reinterpret the social meaning of technologies. Since a variety of technical solutions could potentially fulfill various social objectives, a progressive process of technical change that is responsive to a broad range of human concerns is a possible outcome.

What is the technical code of the Internet? As a "collection of choices by designers, users and policy makers" (Flanagin et al., 2000), the Internet reveals a range of values, mores and social norms. Revisiting the Internet's early history, it is apparent that openness, accessibility and decentralization were purposefully designed into the architecture of ARPANET. This was accomplished by the implementation of TCP/IP protocol, which facilitates a decentralized digital network composed of autonomous nodes (Stevenson 1994). According to Zittrain (2006), the Internet's design embodies both resource limitations and the intellectual interests of its makers. From an engineering perspective, it was desirable that basic network operating protocols were kept simple, which encouraged an elegant and efficient design that could be run easily. Keeping the network's architecture open to future development and growth was also considered desirable. The lack of a central hub or centralized management reflects a social decision: engineers "had little interest in exercising control over the network or its users' behaviour" (p. 1988). Thus both technical and social needs imbricate in the design of the Internet.

What we see here is the condensation of values distinct from those flowing from the profit motive of corporate capitalism into an emergent technical code of the Internet. It is not surprising that the global justice movement embraced the Internet as both its communication medium of choice and its virtual home. A movement of movements, the GJM not only relies on the Internet, it resembles the architecture of the "network of networks" in its nodal, decentralized and horizontal configuration, revealing the dialectical relation between the social and the technical.

TECHNOLOGY AS A 'SCENE OF STRUGGLE'

The turf war in cyberspace is still being waged, with competing goals and interests battling for supremacy. As corporate interests continue to settle the cyberian frontier, the Internet emerges as the locus of a new struggle. Like the Internet itself, this struggle is multilayered. Conflict between private and public interests emerge at the 'content' layer of the Internet, composed of visible elements such as the World Wide Web. Here proprietary and non-proprietary (open-source) software reflect two competing visions of the Internet: the corporate model based on privatization and hence exclusivity; and the community model (Feenberg & Bakardjieva 2004) based on the commons, where sharing gives rise to innovation and creativity. Struggle also occurs in the Internet's underlying infrastructure, at the 'logical' or code layer, which comprises the data transport and transmission protocols. Here corporate interests seek to put an end to network neutrality, an essential component of the Internet's original design based on the principle of common carriage, or the notion that network owners should not be able to discriminate against users of the network (Lessig 2001). Commercial interests are poised to dominate the Web, pushing democratic and public uses to the margins of cyberspace; in addition, corporate influence threatens to further enclose and commodify access to the Internet (Meikle 2002).

The threat lies in the reduction of the "margin of maneuver" of non-commercial users. By "margin of maneuver" is meant the degree of freedom won by the dominated in technical systems that enables them to "work with the 'play' in the system to redefine and modify its forms, rhythms, and purposes" (Feenberg 2002, p. 84). The insidious combination of capitalist intervention at the infrastructural and content layers of the Internet portends an impoverished future for the new medium. Instead of a virtual commons, cyberspace will resemble private property, hemmed in and protected by state and market forces (Lessig 2001).

Feenberg (1991) argues that the technical order is not a mere sum of tools but that it structures the social world. "In choosing our technology we become what we are, which in turn shapes our future choices. The act of choice is technologically embedded and cannot be understood as a free use" (Introduction). But we have some control over the role technology plays in our lives. The future of civilization is not determined by the "immanent drift of technology;" political struggle thus continues to play an important role. This role, however, is tenuous and success is by no means assured. In societies organized around technology, such as modern Western nations, technological power is a foundation of political power.

Against determinism, Feenberg (1991) casts technology not a reified *thing* but as an "ambivalent process of development" (Introduction), one pregnant with both liberating and oppressive possibilities. If technology is a *process*, and not a series of finished products, the chance for intervention, and hence change, exists. The theory of ambivalence cuts through the neutrality claim in attributing social values to the design, and not merely the use, of technical devices and systems. Technology appears not as a destiny, but as "a scene of struggle...a battlefield... in which civilizational alternatives contend" (p. 15). In short, technology has become political and opens new emancipatory potentialities.

THE MICROPOLITICS OF RESISTANCE

Feenberg (2002) argues that the existing society contains the suppressed potentiality for a radical reconstruction of the technological heritage. Actors engaged with technology at the level of design can realize this potentiality for an "alternative modernity." Critical theory of technology thus uncovers the political implications of user agency, showing how new technology can be used to subvert existing social relations, or to create new ones. It does so on the basis of "micropolitics," "a situational politics based on local knowledge and action" (p. 105). This contrasts with the world-historic revolutionary visions imagined by the counterculture of the 1960s. During those contentious times, the technocratic tendency of modern societies was a focal point for political activism. While the hopes of revolution have arguably been dashed, important themes, including racial and gender equality, economic justice, and environmental sustainability, have emerged as central to the global justice movement.

According to Feenberg (2002), the new activism is characterized by small interventions in social life that are numerous and diverse. Despite their humbler scale, these interventions represent moments of agency that could converge to produce long-term subversive impacts. "The tensions in the industrial system can be grasped on a local basis from 'within', by individuals immediately engaged in technically mediated activities and able to actualize ambivalent potentialities suppressed by the prevailing technological rationality" (p. 105). This promises the possibility of rationalizing technology, and hence society, in ways that enhance democracy rather than social control. Democratic rationalization proposes a new sort of agency, wherein members of social groups engage reflexively and dialectically with the technical framework that helps define and organize them (Heidegger, 1977), recognizing themselves—the passive objects of technology—as active subjects capable of redefining the technical order. In starting at the end—with the consequences of technology—it is possible to envision a new beginning.

TECH ACTIVISM'S RADICAL ROOTS

Tech activists in the global justice movement take seriously the idea that 'another world is possible'[2]. They are at the forefront of the drive to shape the Internet into a space and a tool for democratic practice. This current strain of tech activism is the third wave of a movement that emerged in the 1960s as a digital counterculture. Hackers working in the Artificial Intelligence laboratory at Massachusetts Institute for Technology developed the habit of sharing source code based upon a belief that information should be free (Stallman 1999). They were part of a student culture that took up computer networking as a tool of communication. While the New Left "was noisily advocating populist political revolution," observed Brand (in Nelson, 1987) "a tiny sub-subculture of the counterculture was quietly, invisibly fomenting a populist computer revolution..." Among them were the graduate students who largely designed the protocols for ARPANET. Few of these students were part of the countercultural movement in the same manner as radical activists of the day, they shared similar values, such as individual freedom, independent thinking, sharing and cooperation (Castells 2004).

By the 1980s, these values were increasingly marginalized as the computer industry became more and more proprietary. One of the MIT hackers, Richard Stallman, quit the AI lab in 1984 in response to this change and founded the free software movement. This constituted the formalization of a long tradition of openness in the computing community. Ceruzzi (2003) traces the custom of sharing source code to the forming of SHARE, a disparate group of programmers who banded together in 1995 to tackle upgrading their IBM systems.

Stallman (1999) took the principled stance that proprietary software was antisocial and unethical. He challenged the assumption that "we computer users should not care what kind of society we are allowed to have." He began developing an operating system, GNU (Gnu's Not Unix) that was completed with the addition of the Linux kernel in 1992 (gnu.org). The free software movement was based upon four essential freedoms: the freedom to run a program; the freedom to modify a program; the freedom to redistribute copies (either gratis or for a fee); and the freedom to distribute modified versions of the program. Because freedom is considered in the context of knowledge rather than markets, the sharing of source code is not regarded as incompatible with selling a finished program. The crucial point is that the source code—whether in proprietary or free software—always remains freely available.

FREE SOFTWARE VS. OPEN SOURCE

It is freedom, and not simply program development and use, that is the central concern of the free software movement, making it an explicitly political project[3]. According to one tech activist, it comprises"a digital revolution that is social before it is technical" (Obscura, 2005). But some in the programming community refuse to recognize the subversive potential of free software. The Open Source Initiative (OSI), which Eric S. Raymond launched in 1998, is a response to the political or normative approach of the free software movement. Although it assumes an apolitical stance, this movement reveals its bias in its overt support for the status quo.

> The Open Source Initiative does not have a position on whether ideas can be owned, whether patents are good or bad, or any of the related controversies. We think the economic self-interest arguments for open source are strong enough that nobody needs to go on any moral crusades about it... (OSI, *FAQ*).

While the two projects share a similar definition of free software, their objectives are different. Activists in the free software movement focus on the user-technology relationship, implying a critique of some aspects of corporate capitalism. Proponents of the open source program want to facilitate the development of superior software through access to the source code, without addressing capitalist hegemony. Coleman and Hill (2004) note the ease with which free/open source software has been taken up by groups across the political spectrum—from radical activists to liberal reformers to corporations – to facilitate wildly varying objectives. Proponents of open source software dismiss the significance of intentionality, or goal-orientation of the software design, suggesting that what is important about is its "translatability."

In keeping with its business-friendly approach, the Open Source Definition 'logically abandoned all reference to the social and ethical means and motives of free software, not to mention the fight for freedom as a primary aim' (Obscura 2005). The OSI does not disguise its efforts to make free software more compatible with capitalist discourse, describing itself as 'a marketing program for free software. It's a pitch for "free software' on solid pragmatic grounds rather than ideological tub-thumping. The winning substance has not changed, the losing attitude and symbolism have…" (OSI, *FAQ*). For free software advocates, however, the issue is the ethics of software use and development—what Stallman (1999) calls community practice and values. This vision extends beyond the computer industry and embraces the ideal of a just society. According to Stallman, such a challenge to the status quo caused a strong reaction, including hysterical charges of communism against the movement. He explains:

> Talking about freedom, about ethical issues, about responsibilities as well as convenience, is asking people to think about things they might rather ignore. This can trigger discomfort, and some people may reject the idea for that. It does not follow that society would be better off if we stop talking about these things.

In contrast with the Open Source Initiative, the free software movement offers a working example of an alternative social model, one based on decentralization, volunteerism, cooperation and self-empowerment, with the ultimate goal of creating a freer society. It is an example of democratic rationalization, with users redeploying technology (software) to subvert the dominant social order. In this case, democratic control of software suggests a different Internet and, broadly considered, a different world. It is evident, however, that while the free software movement continues to advocate its political program, grounding its position in a critique of capitalism, the broader programming community has drifted away from its more radical origins. Open source software's compatibility with capitalist discourse and practices has been demonstrated in many contexts. But the work of tech activists at Indymedia over more than a decade has challenged this.

SECOND WAVE TECH ACTIVISM: REPOLITICIZING TECHNOLOGY

The free software movement laid the foundation for the third wave of tech activism that began in the late 1990s with the Carnival Against Capital that took place in cities around the world on June 18, 1999. In anticipation of the global day of action, geeks at Community Activist Technology (CAT)[4] developed software that enabled them to stream coverage live to the Internet. This was the precursor to Indymedia's open publishing software, which would end Internet gatekeeping at the content layer. Built into this foundation, though, is the rift that exists between tech activists in the global justice movement and the generally apolitical advocates of open source software development. While both projects share an affinity for collaboration and coordination, with geeks often moving easily between the two, their political, philosophical and technical motivations diverge. Programmers working on open source projects derive satisfaction from the creative expression, intellectual stimulation and improvement of technical skills acquired through programming (Lakhani & Wolf 2005).

Similar benefits may also inspire tech activists in their design and development of the global justice movement's digital infrastructure. But there is no question as to their overarching motivation: "technical means are directed toward political ends" (Coleman 2004). These political ends include the pursuit of social, economic and environmental justice on a global scale. Activists like Alster, a longtime Indymedia geek, identify with the GJM's social justice goals: "I belong to a movement which strives for equal rights (not the written but the real ones) and conditions for all humans (and partially other beings, too) on this planet."[5] In turn, this motivates them to (technical) action. This shift in focus – from developing code for its own sake, for glory, or for money, to hacking for social justice - signals a return to the radical tradition of the free software movement and the repoliticization of computer technology.

Indeed, the reclamation of computer technology as a political frontier is a hallmark of the global justice movement, which seized the world's attention at the 'Battle of Seattle', 1999's massive street protest against the World Trade Organization (WTO). It was here that activists first realized the potential and power of the Internet. While the GJM is part of a continuum of progressive social movements with a long history, the union of such diverse groups and agendas into 'super movement spheres' that organize, mobilize and share information and resources via global, computer-mediated networks marks a shift in radical collective action (Morris & Langman 2002). Thus the GJM is made unique by its truly global scope, enabled largely by the Internet. Tech activists have been central to this movement, facilitating the novel combination of interactive digital technology and social justice activism, and bridging the divide between geek and activist communities. They are responsible for the implementation and continued maintenance of the Independent Media Centre (IMC), perhaps the most prominent example of tech activism.

Also known as Indymedia, this web-based network of radical media-making collectives went live for the Seattle protest. Initially founded to give voice to activists' concerns during the anti-WTO demonstrations, Indymedia became a global platform for the nascent movement. Its use of open publishing software was a radical departure from journalistic tradition. This software allows anyone with Internet access to upload stories to the IMC newswire from anywhere in the world. The elimination of the gatekeeping function by which publishers and editors control access to media messaging offered a challenging alternative to traditional journalism. Subverting the most cherished of journalistic conventions – objectivity - open publishing called upon all witnesses to become reporters, to tell their stories in their own words, and then to publish them on the Internet. "Active," the original open publishing software, was pioneered by the founders of Community Activist Technology in Australia. It is based on Linux, an open source code that is non-proprietary and continually developed by the collective effort of an international community of users. As one of Active's creators observes: "open publishing is the same as free software. They're both (r)evolutionary responses to the privatization of information by multinational monopolies" (Arnison 2002, p. 329). Today, most Indymedia centres run Active, or open publishing software that is based on an Active hack.

THE BIRTH OF INDYMEDIA

There are numerous examples of tech activism, such as the development of activist websites (including features like mailing lists, email accounts, and discussion boards), the refurbishing of old computers for distribution in technology poor areas/nations, and the hosting of hacklabs[6] and other tech training events. Tech activists are also responsible for setting up media centres during major street demonstrations and natural disasters, such as Hurricane Katrina[7]. But Indymedia is arguably the largest and most enduring example of tech activist work carried out under the banner of the global justice movement. The building of the first IMC now approaches legendary status in activist circles. The inaugural post in the days before the "Battle in Seattle" by founding geeks Manse Jacobi and Matthew Arnison, acknowledges the novelty of the new movement. On 24 November 1999, they wrote: "The resistance is global... a trans-pacific collaboration has brought this web site into existence."[8] But it was activists' prior use of the Internet as a communication tool that enabled the global resistance to catalyze such a large scale protest, the likes of which had not been seen in North America since the anti-war movement of the 1960s and early 1970s.

Another geek, Evan Henshaw-Plath, took part in the birth of Seattle IMC during the 1999 protest, writing some of the code that would be incorporated into the open publishing platform that made Indymedia (in)famous. He describes the scene as 'packed and hectic', with techies scrambling to finish the code, shore up the server, and get the website live before the protests began:

> Almost the instant I walked in to the Indymedia Center I had caught the IMC bug. Without knowing the organizing structure, extent of the projects, political background, I could experience the energy. I worked all night on the server and throughout the day of the protests. My experience of the protests was just a half hour when I managed to escape in to the streets...[9]

Since those heady days in Seattle, more than 130 Independent Media Centres have sprung up around the world. According to Sheri Herndon, another Seattle IMC founder, the reason for IMC's initial success was its reliance on openness as a core principle. "When we speak of open publishing it is not just a technological phenomenon; it is a philosophical underpinning that forms a foundation of policy and praxis" (Herndon 2003, p. 2). Indeed, the choice of free software for the implementation of the global site, indymedia.org, was deliberate, and suggests an inheritance from the free software movement, if not direct lineage. It also demonstrates the project's political objectives. At present, all the software on the IMC network is by charter free software.

For more than a decade, free software has enabled the IMC tech collective to develop applications "that encourage cooperation, solidarity, an equal field of participation" (Henshaw-Plath 2002). Some activists extend the metaphor of open source, envisioning it as a model for progressive social organization in a postcapitalist era (Lovink 2003). This sentiment is reflected in a long discussion by the IMC tech collective about the rationale for committing to free software: "It's clear that the technology we use and process by which it's constructed and articulated is deeply political. We are creating the technical systems that prefigure the change we want to see in society" (Henshaw-Plath 2001). Clearly, Indymedia geeks understand coding as a technical means to social ends. While they make an explicit attempt to imbue software with ideals that mirror their social justice goals, they never lose sight of the social purpose of the software.

Indymedia began as a radical media making project dedicated to representing marginalized voices, and opening up public discourse. This was accomplished through the implementation of activist-developed open publishing software, which enabled ordinary citizens to "become the media." This technological innovation contributed to a change in the way users interacted with the Internet, encouraging the shift from passive consumer of news to active producer.

The World Wide Web, as part of the "content" layer of the Internet, is largely dependent upon users—software developers, hackers, corporate entities, governments and "regular" users—for its definition. When the user-technology interface is altered, and new functionalities are added, the web as the face of the Internet is also changed The innovation of blogs, for example, dramatically changed the meaning of the Internet for regular users. Blogs enabled interaction with the www in a novel and dynamic way, providing a platform for creative expression online. The development of plug-n-play blogging software and blog hosting websites in the late 1990s enabled non-technical users to engage with web technology, as both content creators and commentators, causing a proliferation of the phenomenon (Blood 2000). and ultimately giving rise to the social web. By building the digital infrastructure of the global justice movement, tech activists have contributed to the democratization of the Internet, rationalizing it to serve social needs beyond the profit orientation of capitalism. At the same time, these geeks demonstrate insight into the power asymmetries encoded in capitalist socio-technical systems, as well as the knowledge that such asymmetries are both socially constructed and reflective of inequality in the broader social context. With Indymedia, it is apparent that the social and the technical are tightly interwoven; IMC geeks consciously attempt to create a technical environment that promotes equality and democracy, and that, in turn, supports the social change goals of Indymedia and the broader global justice movement.

WILD WILD WIKIS: THE LATEST FRONTIER

Tech activists combat power imbalances in the technical sphere through their development and use of free software. In this way, they carve out their own virtual terrain oriented toward the community model of the Internet, which is based on democratic practice. This model, which contrasts with the commercial model in objectives and orientation, has "profound ethical implications" for the future of the Internet (Feenberg & Bakardjieva 2004, p. 2). Recognizing communication as central to achieving the goals of the global justice movement, activists created their own media system. In the case of the ongoing hacking of Active[10], 'the geeks of IMC-Tech were keenly aware that each technological design or set of features creates a particular publishing structure and, as a result, empowers users…in an equally particular way' (Hill 2003, p. 2). However, it also became apparent that transmitting movement ideals of social, economic and environmental justice to the world through a global digital newswire depended upon internal communication within Indymedia.

The IMC tech collective initially communicated by email lists and Internet Relay Chat (IRC). But by 2002, a number of wikis were set up with the idea of creating a sustainable system for documenting IMC's history and ongoing activities. A wiki is a dynamic website made up of a series of interlinked webpages that can be created and edited by users. As one member of the Docs Tech Working Group observed early on: "Getting a functioning and used wiki is really vital for the network…Email lists just aren't cutting it for the level of organizing and information exchange and growth we need to help facilitate."[11] Techs needed a virtual workspace with a constant online presence, where they could work jointly yet asynchronously, on common projects and tasks. In addition to facilitating workflow, the wiki had the benefit of constructing and cohering an online community of tech activists who identified with the goals of the GJM and worked to provide the technical infrastructure and support the movement required.

Wiki software originated in the mid-1990s in the design pattern community as a means of writing and discussing pattern languages. Ward Cunningham designed and implemented the first wiki engine in 1995. Because of its speed, he named the system wiki-wiki, Hawaiian for "quick." According to Cunningham and Leuf (2001), "a wiki is a freely expandable collection of interlinked Web 'pages', a hypertext system for storing and modifying information—a database where each page is easily editable by any user with a forms-capable Web browser client" (p. 14). All changes are recorded; thus the wiki documents its own history, and stores it for future viewing.

By the end of the 1990s, wikis emerged as a favorable business solution for its ability to facilitate conversational knowledge management via an efficient and collaborative work process (Gonzalez-Reinhart 2005). In the corporate environment, where a competitive edge is paramount, wiki technology promised increased productivity and effectiveness by leveraging employee knowledge. A successful wiki can eliminate the need for other conversational technologies, such as conference calls, emails, discussion forums and instant messaging. As with physical communities, the virtual community created by a wiki fosters socialization and information exchange, which in turn encourage collaborative knowledge creation (ibid).The most famous example of a wiki is Wikipedia, the collaborative online encyclopedia launched in 2001. There are many examples of free and open source wiki engines, including Foswiki, TikiWiki and MediaWiki, on which Wikipedia is built.

For tech activists, building a community that jointly created and maintained knowledge via wiki technology was a breakthrough. But the implications of this new social software were more profound than increased productivity or cost/time savings. In essence, what IMC geeks discovered in the wiki was a new mode of distributed communication. Email and instant messaging facilitate synchronous two-way communication, as with the regular mail or the telephone; but they are typically used for one-to-one communication exchanges rather than group conversation. Pre-Internet computer conferencing systems, such as Usenet and the Bulletin Board System, enabled asynchronous group communication, but were not well suited to the collective production of texts. Wikis, on the other hand, facilitate asynchronous communication amongst multiple distributed users by allowing open editing, content creation and commenting.

Today, web-based discussion forums comprise virtual discussion groups dedicated to common themes or shared interests while electronic email lists constitute a special usage of email that enables widespread dissemination of information. Users subscribe to forums and lists, and receive messages either in the forum or via their private email address. These discussions are theme-based, and allow for interactivity, with subscribers able to post comments that are seen by other subscribers, who may respond in kind. Usually, both Internet forums and email lists are moderated to varying degrees by an administrator, who can set the tone for discussion and the conduct of users. And, as with earlier incarnations of online group communication, they develop exclusive communities, despite the fact that their membership is more or less open. While Internet forums and email lists enable the back-and-forth socialization and exchange of information, neither provides a space for collaborative document development. Posts are not editable, nor do they necessarily build upon one another, even within a single thread (Wagner 2006).

Wikis can be used to communicate with others and exchange information in much the same way as discussion forums and email lists. But uniquely, the software generates a virtual arena for project organization and documentation. Open editing allows for the collective authorship of material, and co-production of the website in a way that other conversational Internet applications do not. The intent is to foster communal development in a virtual space that is owned jointly by all users, and for which all users are responsible. This accounts for the organic nature of a wiki page, in which content changes as users add missing information, correct mistakes and delete erroneous or unnecessary material. In this way, the knowledge jointly produced in a wiki improves incrementally over time. The 'link as you think' feature, whereby users create links to existing and potential pages in a wiki, is one example of this process.

Wikis rely on a simplified markup language—character combinations for formatting and linking documents—rather than HTML, which is the predominant markup language of the World Wide Web. This allows users without programming skills the ability to link pages and format textual content. When writing an entry, users enhance their content by linking to pages containing more in depth information using WikiWords (multiple words capitalized and concatenated). Thus linking becomes an intuitive act, based on the meaning a contributor is trying to convey. Users are encouraged to insert WikiWords whenever possible, as rich linking contributes to the wiki's success. A question mark accompanies links to pages that have not yet been created, inviting other users to contribute the missing information and encouraging collaborative knowledge production.

This "link as you think" feature is a deliberate design element that fosters the creation of a shared language. As discussed above, this shared language emerges spontaneously and is fundamental to the effectiveness of a wiki. "Shared language is an absolute prerequisite for collaboration. The lack of shared language is the most common roadblock to effective collaboration, be it a small work team or a community of thousands" (Kim 2005). Referring to a page by name encourages the author be reflective, to consider more closely the term that best represents it to the audience for whom s/he is writing. As one tech activist puts it, the "link as you think" feature is "a way of building a community-specific vocabulary that allows you to easily formulate complex thoughts by using the terms your community thinks are important" (Schroeder 2005).

This often occurs through "namespace clash." A namespace provides context for, and contains, the names in a wiki (and on the Internet in general), which has to be unique when concatenated to form a URL. The process of creating WikiWords (and thus new links to pages within the wiki) is a naming convention that creates conflict amongst users. Namespace clash can be positive as it leads to nomenclature convergence—users adopting a shared terminology—an process that can also generate serendipitous connections within a wiki.

FROM TWIKI TO FOSWIKI: THE EVOLUTION OF A WIKI

Indymedia made early use of wiki technology for the Global Indymedia Documentation Project, which gathers collective knowledge about IMC's history, its current role(s) and its short and longterm goals. Documentation is vital to the success of Indymedia; not only does it provide a public record, it creates a fluidity that facilitates participation at varying levels. The Indymedia Documentation Project "looks like a normal Web site...except that it encourages contribution and *editing* of pages, questions, answers, comments and updates" (IMC, *WelcomeGuest*). Importantly, users are not required to know complex code in order to add, change or delete content, opening up participation to a much wider demographic than is usual on the Internet. Wiki technology was appealing because of its ability to facilitate information flow, allowing distributed teams to work together seamlessly and productively, and eliminating the one-webmaster syndrome of centralized control and outdated content.

In 2002, IMC techs adopted TWiki, a free software wiki clone aimed at the corporate intranet world. TWiki assembles a number of separately running wikis in one website, docs.indymedia.org. It was one of the largest TWiki installations on the World Wide Web until 2009, when the the documentation project migrated to Foswiki[12]. The Indymedia Documentation Project wiki is a vast repository of information arranged into different "webs." Each web within the wiki is organized by topic, such as Global, Local, Tech, People and Groups. Each web contains policy documents, proposals, projects research papers, and meeting logs of concern to its topic, providing an online space for exploring a range of issues that are critical to the smooth running of the network, both technical and social, as well as at the regional and global levels. The Documentation Project is both an archive of Indymedia's, creating an invaluable store of cumulative knowledge developed over the last decade and a dynamic space in which IMC volunteers continue to evolve and enhance the project. The wiki's dynamism is apparent in the "What's New" link to the recent changes page and the comments at the bottom of any give page, both of which document ongoing contributions.

While the wiki opened up a new mode of communication for IMC volunteers, and the tech activists who maintain Indymedia's digital infrastructure, it is not without challenges. In fact, the IMC Docs Project was read-only (editing function disabled) from March-September 2006. This, however, had more to do with deeper problems plaguing Indymedia as a globally distributed, volunteer-run collective, including activist burnout and conflict over best practices, than shortcomings in the wiki technology itself[13]. In December 2009, the server crashed, and the Documentation Project wiki was offline for two months, and read-only until June 2009. Once again, unforeseeable technical difficulties and the challenge of relying on volunteer labour contributed to the wiki's lack of functionality. That IMC Techs continued the wiki project after such a major interruption reveals the compatibility of the affordances built into wiki technology including openness and trustworthiness, which in turn encourage sharing, cooperation, collaboration and democratic communication.

A common concern about the openness of wikis is the fear of vandals who delete or deface content, either in sport, from spite or for commercial gain. For example, wikis are a common target for spammers seeking to promote products or websites. Indeed, the open philosophy does not defend against ill-intentioned users, despite the fact that many wikis require some form of user validation or registration, block new or anonymous users from certain pages or operations, or use a CAPTCHA test to authenticate human users. Wikis are designed to make it easy to correct mistakes (rather than making it difficult to make them), thereby providing ways to ensure the validity of content despite the ease of modifications. Most wikis have a "Recent Changes" page that records the latest edits, or all changes made within a specific timeframe. "Revision History" shows previous page versions, and the "dif feature" highlights the changes between two versions. This allows users to deal swiftly with attacks such as wiki spam or vandalism, correcting any malicious modifications or restoring older, more appropriate content. On a small wiki, it takes more effort to vandalize a page than to revert it to an acceptable version, which can be done with one click of the mouse. On a large wiki installation, like the IMC Docs Project, wiki vandalism can be much more problematic, creating daily, tedious work. In either case, the 'infinite undo' function ensures that no operation is ever permanently destructive (Lih 2004, p. 10). This "soft security" approach is intended to protect the system and its users in "gentle and unobtrusive ways…It works architecturally in defense to convince people against attacking and to limit damage. It works socially in offense to convince people to be friendly and to get out of the way of people adding value" (MeatballWiki 2006). The result is an often invisible barrier to counteract "graffiti" after the fact, after it has appeared.

Despite these proactive measures, some skeptics are not convinced of the ability of wikis to contribute to the development of a community model of the Internet. Feenberg and Bakardjieva (2004) contend that it is not enough for Internet groupware to sustain values such as free speech, universal participation, mutual aid and information sharing; they must also support the technical conditions needed to foster online community. These conditions they find in the first virtual communities organized on pre-Internet computer conferencing systems and BBSs, and include forming closed communities, tracking participation, archiving community discussions and affirming participant identities. Clearly, a closed group in which members' presence is visible to each other, their common past accessible, and their true identity secured offers a favourable environment in which to display such moral qualities as loyalty, civility and the other virtues of community (p. 7).

But a well-functioning wiki addresses these concerns, despite—or perhaps because of—its open nature. Wikis coalesce around common projects, and tend to attract only those interested in developing those projects. In discussing the development of the virtual community that arose around the Indymedia Documentation Project wiki, Intrigeri (2006) noted: "It took time, conflicts, energy, love, patience and a one-week real-life meeting to build a collective, to build common practice and ways to communicate, in order to be able to work together in a cool and efficient way." In order to gain editing privileges, users are often required to create an account or register to a wiki, and even if they become known only by their "nom du Net," they develop online identities, and can build online relationships with other collaborators in the wiki based on trust and a common objective. Anti-social, aggressive or otherwise destructive behaviour typically is not tolerated in a well-functioning wiki, where the community works diligently to maintain and protect the quality of collectively produced content. Wikipedia, with its legions of Wikipedians—people who write, edit, fact check and protect from vandalism the millions of chapters—is a good example of this.

THE EMANCIPATORY POWER OF WIKIS?

What are the implications of wikis for tech activism in today's global justice movement? Glaser (2004) assesses the emancipatory power of wikis, concluding that participating in a wiki is a political act with implications that can extend beyond cyberspace. The egalitarian structure of the wiki is based on decentralization of authority and horizontal self-organization. Like Indymedia, wherein the gatekeeping power of editors and news producers to control the flow of information is obliterated, "wikis are administered by a group of people with equal rights who control each other and whose work and decisions are subject to all users' discussion" (p. 4). In other words, there are no gatekeepers in a wiki.

Wiki's egalitarian structure is characteristic of the global justice movement, which eschews formal leadership and is configured rhizomatically in loose networks of autonomous nodes. Decentralization of power is critical for undermining social hierarchies that characterize modern capitalist societies, where the few rule over the many. In modern Western capitalism, this elite minority typically dominates the production of information while the majority of people are relegated to the passive and disempowered role of perpetual consumers. In a wiki, there are no access barriers: as with Indymedia, producers of content can also be its consumers, and vice versa.

The elimination of access barriers facilitates participation in wikis, as does the purposely designed ease-of-use. "As you edit there is very little to get in the way of clear thinking and writing…The easier we can make a wiki to use, the more participants we can attract and the greater the value of the system" (Cunningham n.d.). The simplified markup language enhances usability by eliminating the need for a webmaster and allowing users with no programming skills to contribute to the wiki. Participation is further enhanced by the self-organization that wikis require, which in turn leads to self-control. "Everybody feels that they have a sense of responsibility because anybody can contribute" (ibid.). A community can grow up around well-used wikis, and users are invested in keeping their wiki relevant and functional. As discussed above, this is largely due to the collective production of content. In the process of organizing their wiki, users can discover shared interests and begin work on common projects that reflect the concerns and needs of the community, and that can promote social cohesion in the virtual environment.

Key to working collaboratively is the feedback generated through the wiki's interactivity. Unlike the dominant communication technologies of radio and television, the Internet is highly interactive. Building upon this functionality, wiki software enables not only adding comments to existing content, as in a weblog, chatroom or email exchange, but the complete restructuring of the entire website, including its deletion. If modifications are not deemed an improvement, however, they are quickly "undone" by other users.

Wikis are a social and organizational phenomenon that contrast with the current model of society, organized around neoliberal globalization, and prefigures alternative conceptions of social organization. Considered thus, their subversive political implications are clear. The process of refining and defending views in a collaborative context leads to a deeper understanding of complex ideas, an understanding with the potential for application in the "real world." As Glaser (2004) observers, "the recognition of this might lead some people to take the organization of work in a wiki as a model that could succeed in the real world as well" (p. 7). The "wiki way" of self-organization and collaboration can produce high quality work without capitalist incentives like competition or profit. It thus reveals other ways to live with and value technology not currently embraced by the dominant social order.

It becomes clear how wiki software facilitates the formation of online communities that coalesce around a common interest and a shared language, resulting in a super-linear (exponential) model of knowledge production (Wagner 2006). The openness that characterizes the wiki is its strength, rather than an apparent weakness. According to Cunningham (n.d.), trustworthiness is a principle that inspired his initial wiki design and it is built into the software's technical code: "this is at the core of wiki. Trust the people, trust the process, enable trust-building."[14] Wikis encourage trust because their ability to function is based on the assumption that participants have good intentions; the open-ended power to add, delete or alter content makes a wiki vulnerable, and dependent upon ethical conduct. Thus, as with any functional community, a successful wiki is heavily reliant on norms of social behaviour.

This resonates with tech activists, for whom the wiki as an online community offers the chance to live the social change they seek in the broader society. Democracy, equality and justice can switch from being abstract ideals to concrete social practices. At the same time, wiki software is part of the digital infrastructure tech activists build and maintain in order to achieve more immediate movement goals, and as such it represents only one tool in the activists' repertoire of contestation. Considered thus, wikis emerge as an ideal mode of communication for a distributed network such as the global justice movement, where participants from disparate geographical locales, with varying skill and commitment levels, as well as ethnic, class and technical backgrounds, work together toward a shared vision of a better world.

CONCLUSION

The Internet remains an unfinished and contested technology still subject to intervention and transformation by users. Tech activists in the global justice movement bridge the divide between geek and activist communities, developing and maintaining a digital infrastructure that supports progressive activism on a planetary scale. Through their free software work, tech activists deliberately oppose the commercial take-over of cyberspace and adapt it to democratic purposes. In the case of Indymedia, tech activists redeployed wiki software to facilitate movement goals – by creating a public space for online collaboration, and by challenging inherent power inequities reflected in the broader society. The Documentation Project wiki's open and decentralized structure mirrors that of the global justice movement (and aspects of the Internet's construction, for that matter) and remains in direct opposition to dominant societal norms based on capitalist hegemony. It is a social software that enables and may also prefigures progressive social change, hinting at more egalitarian, humane ways of organizing our modern industrial world. Does this indicate, or contribute to, a radical reform of the technical sphere? It remains to be seen. But it certainly offers hope that, indeed, another world is possible.

NOTES

[1] There is a considerable literature on this phenomenon. See Bennett, 2004; Diebert, 2000; Kahn & Kellner, 2004; Meikle, 2002; Smith, 2001; van Aelst & Wlagrave, 2004.

[2] Taken as the official slogan for the 2001 World Social Forum, this phrase has become something of a rallying cry for the global justice movement. It is not a vision of a specific other world, as Naomi Klein (2001) astutely observes, simply the idea that, in theory, another one could exist. This contradicts the truism of capitalist hegemony, which states that the current socio-economic configuration of modern Western society is the only possible one, its flaws notwithstanding.

[3] Another political project founded in defense of freedom on the Internet is the Electronic Frontier Foundation. Begun in 1990, the EFF works to protect the public interest in legal battles over digital rights in cyberspace. A discussion of this group, however, is beyond the scope of this essay. See www.eff.org.

[4] Interview with CAT founder and tech activist Matthew Arnison, 2003.

[5] Personal communication with Alster, 2 December 2005.

[6] Hacklabs are political spaces (often temporary) that provide community computer and Internet access. They are used for independent media, the promotion of free software and other emancipatory technologies. Here tech activists share skills with one another and the broader public. For example, see www.hacklab.org.

[7] In Houston, Indymedia and low power FM radio activists set up a disaster information radio station. New Orleans IMC offered breaking coverage and activists set up a media centre in Algers, a portion of the city that did not flood from the levee breaches. IMC USA created a topical site, Katrina.indymedia.us.org, which carried news from across the Indymedia network (http://www. anarchogeek.com/chapters/category/indymedia).

[8] For the full transcript, visit http://seattle.indymedia.org/en/1999/11/2.shtml.

[9] Interview with Evan Henshaw-Plath, 28 July 2003.

[10] See Hill (2003) for a history of open publishing software development within IMC.

[11] John Windmueller posting a comment to the Indymedia Documentation Project Wiki, http://docs. indymedia.org/view/Sysadmin/ImcDocsReplaceWikiEngine.

[12] After a server crash in December 2008, IMC Techs decided to migrate docs.indymedia.org to Foswiki, a fork of the Twiki project. The majority of Twiki developers left in October 2008 due to the abandonment of a democratic governance model in favor of a Benevolent Dictator For Life (BDFL). See http://slashdot.org/firehose.pl?op=view&id=1339353

[13] Interview with Indymedia tech activist Garcon du Monde (gdm), 2005.

[14] For more on Ward Cunningham's wiki design principles, see http://c2.com/cgi/wiki? WikiDesignPrinciples.

REFERENCES

Abbate, J. (1999). *Inventing the Internet*. MIT Press, Cambridge, MA.

Arnison, M. (2002). Open publishing. *Sarai Reader 2002: The Cities of Everyday Life*, 329–333.

Bennett, W.L. (2004). Communicating global activism: Strengths and vulnerabilities of networked politics. In W. van de Donk, B.D. Loader, P.G. Nixon & D. Rucht, (Eds.) *Cyberprotest: New media, citizens, and social movements*. London and New York: Routledge.

Blood, Rebecca. (2000). *Weblogs: A history and perspective*. Retrieved June 30, 2011 from http://www.rebeccablood.net/essays/weblog_history.html

Castells, Manuel. (2001). *The Internet galaxy: Reflections on the Internet, business, and society*. New York : Oxford University Press.

Ceruzzi, P. (2003). *A history of modern computing.* 2nd edn. Cambridge, MA: MIT Press.

Coleman, Biella. (2004). Indymedia's independence: From activist media to free Software. *PlaNetwork Journal, 1*(1). Retrieved November 22, 2006 from http://journal.planetwork.net/chapter. php?lab=coleman0704.

Coleman, Biella, & Hill, Mako. (2004). How free became open and everything else under the sun. *MC: A Journal of Media and Culture.* Retrieved 11 August 2004 from http://journal.media-culture.org.au/0406/02_Coleman-Hill.php

Cunningham, Ward. (n.d.). *Why wiki works.* Retrieved 11 August 2006. http://www.c2.com/cgi/wiki?WhyWikiWorks & Leuf, Bo. (2001). *The Wiki way.* Boston, MA: Addison-Wesley.

Deibert, R. J. (2000). International plug 'n' play? Citizen activism, the Internet and global public policy. *International Studies Perspectives, 1,* 255–272.

Edwards, P. N. (2003). Infrastructure and modernity: Force, time and social organization in the history of sociotechnical systems. In T. J. Misa, P. Brey & A. Feenberg (Eds.) *Modernity and technology.* Cambridge, MA : MIT Press.

Feenberg, A. (2005). Critical theory of technology: An overview. *Tailoring Biotechnologies, 1*(1), 47–64.

-- (2002). *Transforming technology: A critical theory revisited.* Oxford and New York: Oxford University Press.

(1999). *Questioning technology.* London and New York: Routledge.

-- (1995). *Alternative modernity: The technical turn in philosophy and social theory.* Berkeley, CA: University of California Press.

-- (1991). *Critical theory of technology.* New York: Oxford University Press.'Introduction' retrieved 18 November 2005 from http://www-rohan.sdsu.edu/faculty/feenberg/CRITSAM2.HTM.

& Bakardjieva, M. (2004). Consumers or citizens? The online community debate. In A. Feenberg and D. Barney (Eds.) *Community in the digital age: Philosophy and practice.* Lanham: Rowman & Littlefield.

Flanagin, A.J., Farinola, Wendy Jo, & Metzger, M.J. (2000). The technical code of the Internet/World Wide Web. *Critical Studies in Media Communication,* 17(4), 409–428.

Glaser, Anja Ebersbach-Markus. (2004). Towards emancipatory use of a medium: The Wiki. *International Journal of Information Ethics, 2,* 1–9. Retrieved 5 December 2005 from http://www.i-r-i-e.net/inhalt/002/ijie_002_09_ebersbach.pdf.

GNU. (n.d.) *Overview of the GNU system.* Retrieved 22 November 2005 from http://www.gnu.org/gnu/gnu-history.html.

Gonzolez-Reinhart, Jennifer. (2005). Wiki and the wiki way: Beyond a knowledge management system. *Information Systems Research Center.* University of Houston.

Hafner, K., & Lyon, M. (1996). *Where wizards stay up late: The origins of the internet.* New York: Simon & Schuster.

Heidegger, Martin. (1977). *The question concerning technology, and other essays.* Trans. by William Lovitt. New York: Harper & Row.

Henshaw-Plath, Evan. (2002). *Proposal to reform www.indy by highlighting local IMCs.* Retrieved 29 April 2003 from http://internal.indymedia.org/front.php3?chapter_id=538

(2001). *IMC-Tech summary for November 16th 2001.* Retrieved 28 November 2005from http://archives.lists.indymedia.org/imc-summaries/2001-November/000028.html.

Herndon, Sheri. (2003). *Barranquilla Presentation/Notes: IMC Panel.* Retrieved 1 October 2007 http://www.ourmedianet.org/papers/om2003/herndron_om3.rtf

Hill, Mako. (2003). *Software, politics and Indymedia.* Retrieved 25 November 2005 from http://mako.cc/writing/mute-indymedia_software.html.

Indymedia. (nd) *WelcomeGuest.* Retrieved June 30, 2011 from http://docs.indymedia.org/

Intrigeri. (2006) *How to build or destroy collective desire and practice.* Retrieved 1 October 2007 from http://lists.indymedia.org/pipermail/imc-docs/2006-August/0830-za.html

Kahn, R.V., & Kellner, D. (2004). *Virtually democratic: Online communities and Internet activism.* In A. Feenberg & D. Barney (Eds.) Community in the digital age: Philosophy and practice. Lanham: Rowman and Littlefield.

Kim, E. E. (2005). *The brilliant essence of wikis.* Retrieved 21 September 2005 from http://www.eekim. com/blog/2005/09/.

Klein, Naomi. (2001). World Social Forum: A fete for the end of history. *The Nation.* March 19, 2001. Retrieved 23 November 2005 from http://www.nadir.org/nadir/initiativ/agp/free/wsf/fete.htm.

(2004). Reclaiming the commons. In Tom Mertes (Ed.) *A movement of movements: Is another world really possible?* London & New York: Verso.

Lakhani, K.R. & Wolf, R.G. (2005). Why hackers do what they do: Understanding motivation and effort in free/open source software projects. In J. Feller, B. Fitzgerald, S. Hissam & K.R. Lakhani (Eds.) *Perspectives on free and open source software.* Cambridge, MA: MIT Press.

Lemley, M. A. & Lessig, L. (2004). The end of end-to-end: Preserving the architecture of the Internet in the broadband era. In Mark N. Cooper (Ed.) Open architecture as communications policy. Stanford, CA: Stanford Law School. Retrieved 21 November from http://cyberlaw.stanford.edu/blogs/ cooper/archives/openarchitecture.pdf.

Lessig, L. (2001). The Internet under siege. *Foreign Policy,* November/ December, 2001. Retrieved 22 July 2003 from http://www.lessig.org/content/columns/foreignpolicy1.pdf.

(1999). *Code and other laws of cyberspace.* New York: Basic Books.

Lih, Andrew. (2004). *The foundations of participatory journalism and the Wikipedia Project.* Paper presented at Association for Education in Journalism and Mass Communication, Toronto, Canada, 7 August 2004. Retrieved 10 November 2005 from http://jmsc.hku.hk/faculty/alih/publications/aejmc-2004-final-forpub-3.pdf.

Lovink, Geert. (2003). *My first recession.* Rotterdam, The Netherlands: V2_/Nai Publishers.

McCaughey, M., & Ayers, M.D. (2003). *Cyberactivism: Online activism in theory and Practice.* New York: Routledge.

Meatball Wiki. (2006). *SoftSecurity.* Retrieved 14 August 2007 from http://www.usemod.com/cgi-bin/mb.pl?SoftSecurity

Meikle, G. (2002). *Future active: Media activism and the Internet.* New York: Routledge.

Morris, D., & Langman, L. (2002). *Networks of dissent: A typology of social movements in a global age.* Paper presented at International Workshop on Community Informatics, Montreal, Canada, 8 October 2002. Retrieved 2 December 2005 from http://www.is.njit.edu/vci/iwci/iwci1-toc.html

Nelson, T. H. (1987). *Computer lib: Dream machines.* Redmond, WA: Tempus Books.

Obscura, V. (2005). *From free software to street activism and vice versa: An Introduction.* Retrieved 25 November 2005 from http://garlicviolence.org/txt/drkvg-fs2sa.html.

Open Source Initiative. (n.d.) *FAQ.* Retrieved 15 April 2007 from http://www.opensource.org/advocacy/faq.php.

Pinch, T. & Bijker, W.E. (1987). The social construction of facts and artifacts: Or how the sociology of science and the sociology of technology might benefit each other. In W.E. Bijker, T. Hughes & T. Pinch, (Eds.) *The social construction of technological systems.* Cambridge, MA: MIT Press.

Rheingold, H. (1993). *The virtual community: Homesteading on the electronic frontier.* Reading, MA: Adison-Wesley.

Schroeder, A. (2005). *Comment: The brilliant essence of wikis.* Retrieved 21 September 2005 from http://www.eekim.com/blog/2005/09/.

Smith, J. (2001). Cyber subversion in the information economy. *Dissent,* Spring, 48–52.

Stallman, R. (1999). *The GNU Project.* Retrieved 22 November 2005 from http://www.gnu.org/gnu/ thegnuproject.html.

Stevenson, J. H. (2001). *(De)constructing the matrix: Toward a social history of the early internet.* Retrieved February 13,2005 from http://www.tranquileye.com/netessays/de_constructing_the_ matrix.html van Aelst, P., & Walgrave, S. (2004). New media, new movements? The role of the Internet in shaping the "anti-globalization" movement. In W. van de Donk, B.D. Loader, P.G. Nixon & D. Rucht (Eds.) *Cyberprotest: New media, citizens, and social movements*. London and New York: Routledge.

Tidwell, Alan. (1999). The virtual agora: dialogues and professional communities. *First Monday*. Retrieved 1 October 2007 from http://www.firstmonday.dk/issues/issue4_7/tidwell/index.html

Wagner, C. (2006). Breaking the knowledge acquisition bottleneck through conversational knowledge management. *Information Resources Management Journal, 19*(1).

Zittrain, Jonathon L. (2006). The generative Internet. *Harvard Law Review, 119*, 1974–2040.

INDEX

Printed in the United States
By Bookmasters